Overview Map Key

Part 1: South
OREGON BORDER TO WHITE PA

Part 2: Central
WHITE PASS TO STEVENS PASS

Part 3: North
STEVENS PASS TO CANADIAN BORDER

(Continued on next page)

Overview Map Key *(continued)*

DAY & SECTION HIKES

Pacific Crest Trail

WASHINGTON

ADRIENNE SCHAEFER

2ND EDITION

 WILDERNESS PRESS . . . *on the trail since 1967*

Day & Section Hikes Pacific Crest Trail: Washington
Copyright © 2017 by Adrienne Schaefer
All rights reserved
Printed in the United States of America
Published by Wilderness Press
Distributed by Publishers Group West
Second edition, first printing

Library of Congress Cataloging-in-Publication Data

Names: Schaefer, Adrienne, 1979– author.
Title: Day & section hikes Pacific Crest Trail : Washington / [by Adrienne Schaefer].
Other titles: Day and section hikes Pacific Crest Trail
Description: Second Edition. | Birmingham, Alabama : Wilderness Press . . . On the Trail Since 1967, [2017]
    | "Distributed by Publishers Group West"—T.p. verso.
Identifiers: LCCN 2017030898 | ISBN 978-0-89997-836-9 (paperback) | ISBN 978-0-89997-837-6 (e-book)
Subjects: LCSH: Hiking—Washington (State)—Guidebooks. | Hiking—Pacific Crest Trail—Guidebooks.
    Trails—Washington (State)—Guidebooks. | Washington (State)—Guidebooks. | Pacific Crest Trail—
    Guidebooks.
Classification: LCC GV199.42.W2 P3433 2017 | DDC 796.5109797—dc23
LC record available at lccn.loc.gov/2017030898

Project editor: Ritchey Halphen
Cartography and cover design: Scott McGrew
Photos: Adrienne Schaefer, except where noted
Text design: Ian Szymkowiak/Palace Press International, with updates by Annie Long
Copy editor: Kerry J. Smith
Proofreader: Rebecca Henderson
Indexer: Sylvia Coates

🐾 WILDERNESS PRESS

An imprint of AdventureKEEN
2204 First Ave. S., Ste. 102
Birmingham, AL 35233
800-443-7227, fax 205-326-1012

Visit wildernesspress.com for a complete listing of our books and for ordering information. Contact us at our website, at facebook.com/wildernesspress1967, or at twitter.com/wilderness1967 with questions or comments. To find out more about who we are and what we're doing, visit blog.wildernesspress.com.

Front cover: Snowgrass Flats in Goat Rocks Wilderness; photo by Spring Images/Alamy Stock Photo; (inset) on the Pacific Crest Trail near Harts Pass; photo by TMI / Alamy Stock Photo

SAFETY NOTICE Although Wilderness Press and Adrienne Schaefer have made every attempt to ensure that the information in this book is accurate at press time, they are not responsible for any loss, damage, injury, or inconvenience that may occur to anyone while using this book—you are responsible for your own safety and health while in the wilderness. Be aware that trail conditions can change from day to day. Always check local conditions, know your own limitations, and consult a map.

TABLE OF CONTENTS

(*Continued on next page*)

PART 2: CENTRAL

WHITE PASS TO STEVENS PASS (continued)

PART 3: NORTH

STEVENS PASS TO CANADIAN BORDER   147

DEDICATION

For my family—I love you all and thank you for your support.

ACKNOWLEDGMENTS

I WOULD FIRST LIKE TO THANK my husband, John, for supporting me through all of the ups and downs of this bumpy adventure. I would also like to thank our two boys, Tye and Reid, for sitting through all of my pictures whenever I would return from a hike and being on their "best" behavior when I was gone. I am forever grateful to both my parents for supporting me through all of my crazy endeavors, and I owe my mom special thanks for hiking on trails that she would rather have read about.

This book would have never happened if it hadn't been for Amanda and Judy Ford discovering this opportunity for me and encouraging me to pursue it. Tyler and Lindsay Kellet get special recognition for spending a semihypothermic afternoon on Little Giant Pass with me, and their words of advice helped make this book what it is.

Numerous folks kept me company on the trails, including Aaron Sherred, Mike and Maurisa Descheemaeker, Reggie Descheemaeker, Rebecca Lofgren, Terri, Stacy, Jen Glyzenski, Carla, Dani Reynaud, and Abby Pattison. Thank you to the crew from Carlton, John Jorgenson, Surya and Bhavesh Dimodica, and Zeke and Kathleen Hirschstein for sharing their amazing garden (are you sure it's organic?) and their homes with me.

My good friends at Mount Rainier National Park kept me entertained on rest days, and Rebecca A., Andy, and Barry (my saving grace up at Three Lakes) made me feel right at home. While I'm a country bumpkin at heart, there's nothing quite like a night of good wine and great food after a day's hike; thanks to Bob and Sarah White for a memorable weekend in Portland. When I couldn't drag anyone out, I could always count on my parents' dog,

Maggie, to join me. Come rain or shine, her enthusiasm to be out was contagious. I couldn't have done the second edition if it weren't for my dog, Lemah, who helped me carry all sorts of stuff into the Pasayten and Glacier Peak Wilderness Areas.

Thank you to all the men and women who braved the mountains when they were truly wild and who laid the foundation for what we have today. My hiking experiences would not have been nearly as enjoyable if not for the hard work of the National Park Service and U.S. Forest Service employees who maintain our roads, trails, and bridges.

I could not have researched, written about, or hiked these trails without the help of countless other resources, including Dr. Fred T. Darvill Jr.'s *Hiking the North Cascades;* Ira and Vicky Spring and Harvey Manning's 100 Hikes series; Chester Marler's *East of the Divide;* Andy Selters's *Pacific Crest Trail: Oregon and Washington,* also published by Wilderness Press; and the wonderful people at the Washington Trails Association who posted trip updates online. Their words were truly inspiring.

To all of the other people who touched my life in one way or another during this incredible journey through the Washington Cascades, thank you.

—*Adrienne Schaefer*

PREFACE

JUST OUTSIDE MOUNT ST. HELENS National Volcanic Monument lies the small town of Cougar, Washington. It's your typical mountain town, complete with a diner, tavern, convenience store, and two RV parks. Normally I would continue down the road to a more primitive site, but exhaustion prevailed, and the next thing I knew I was driving by the neon flashing vacancy light of an RV park.

I knocked on the door and was immediately greeted by a friendly couple. They invited me into their home, and I told them I was looking for a tent site. They gave me a quick head-to-toe, and I suddenly became aware of how I must look: my legs covered with a thick coat of dust; my hair matted from too many days under a hat; my clothes a wrinkled, dirty mess. The woman spoke first, saying, "Well, it looks like you need to treat yourself to a good night's sleep." I informed her that I was on a budget, but she waved her hand, telling me not to worry. The next thing I knew, I was unlocking the door to a sweet little cabin with clean towels in hand.

Throughout my time exploring the Pacific Crest Trail (PCT) in Washington State, spontaneous moments like this were part of what made my trips so memorable. Whether it was fresh goat cheese from a gardener in Stehekin, homemade honey from a street vendor in Hood River, colorful veggies from the Twisp Farmers Market, or a hot cup of espresso from the hardware store in Plain, each mountain community surrounding the PCT had something unique to offer.

This book is a culmination of my experiences along a trail full of culture, history, and breathtaking scenery. Selecting my favorite hikes was no easy task. Like the communities that surround the PCT, each trail offers something special that sets it apart from the others. I found myself on numerous occasions saying, "I had no idea this place was so beautiful. This hike is definitely going in the book!" Or perhaps it was a bit of history that caught my attention, such as finding an old sheepherder trail or seeing the remnants of an abandoned fire lookout. In the end, I whittled them down to

33 spectacular hikes that stretched from the mighty waters of the Columbia River to the majestic peaks of the North Cascades.

The actual task of hiking all the trails was no easy feat. (I would be lying if I said my trip to Chain Lakes in a torrential downpour was a highlight of my hiking career.) But as time fades, memories of napping on sunbaked rocks, taking a dunk in alpine lakes, or watching alpenglow dance on snow-capped peaks replaces those less desirable moments.

This book will inspire you to discover a side of Washington State that you may have never seen, whether you've lived here your whole life or you're just passing through. Hike with open eyes, and your journey through this beautifully diverse state will bring you as much fulfillment as I experienced while hiking these trails.

RECOMMENDED HIKES

RECOMMENDED HIKES

RECOMMENDED HIKES

Dewey Lake (see Hike 10, page 78)

INTRODUCTION

How to Use This Guidebook

THE FOLLOWING SECTION walks you through this book's organization, making it easy and convenient to plan great hikes.

The Overview Map, Map Key, and Legend

Use the overview map on the inside front cover to assess the exact locations of each hike's primary trailhead. Each hike's number appears on the overview map, on the map key facing the overview map, in the table of contents, and at the beginning of each hike profile.

The book is organized into three regions. The hikes within each region are noted as out-and-back day hikes, loop and semiloop day hikes, and overnight hikes in the map key (pages i–ii) and the table of contents. A legend that details the symbols found on trail maps appears on the inside back cover.

Trail Maps

In addition to the overview map on the inside cover, a detailed map of each hike's route appears with its profile. On each of these maps, symbols indicate the trailhead, the complete route, significant features, facilities, and topographic landmarks such as creeks, overlooks, and peaks.

To produce the highly accurate maps in this book, I used a Garmin eTrex GPS unit to gather data while hiking each route, then sent that data to Wilderness Press's expert cartographers. Be aware, though, that your GPS device is no substitute for sound, sensible navigation that takes into account the conditions that you observe while hiking.

Further, despite the high quality of the maps in this guidebook, the publisher and myself strongly recommend that you always carry an additional map, such as the ones noted in each profile opener's "Maps" entry.

Elevation Profiles

Each hike also contains a detailed elevation profile that augments the trail map. The elevation profile provides a quick look at the trail from the side, enabling you to visualize how the trail rises and falls. Key points along the way are labeled. Note the number of feet between each tick mark on the vertical axis, or height scale. The height scales provide an accurate assessment of each hike's climbing difficulty, so that flat hikes don't seem steep and vice versa.

GPS Trailhead Coordinates

As noted in "Trail Maps" on the previous page, I used a handheld GPS unit to obtain geographic data and sent the information to the publisher's cartographers. In the opener for each hike profile, the coordinates—the intersection of latitude (north) and longitude (west)—will orient you from the trailhead. In some cases, you can drive within viewing distance of a trailhead. Other hiking routes require a short walk to the trailhead from a parking area.

This guidebook expresses GPS coordinates in degree–decimal minute format. The latitude–longitude grid system is likely quite familiar to you, but here's a refresher, pertinent to visualizing the coordinates:

Imaginary lines of latitude—called *parallels* and approximately 69 miles apart from each other—run horizontally around the globe. The equator is established to be 0°, and each parallel is indicated by degrees from the equator: up to 90°N at the North Pole and down to 90°S at the South Pole.

Imaginary lines of longitude—called *meridians*—run perpendicular to latitude lines. Longitude lines are likewise indicated by degrees. Starting from 0° at the Prime Meridian in Greenwich, England, they continue to the east and west until they meet 180° later at the International Date Line in the Pacific Ocean. At the equator, longitude lines also are approximately 69 miles apart, but that distance narrows as the meridians converge toward the North and South Poles.

As an example, the GPS coordinates for Hike 1, Gillette Lake (page 24), are as follows: **N45° 39.110' W121° 55.888'.**

For more on GPS technology, visit usgs.gov or refer to Steve Hinch's *Outdoor Navigation with GPS* (Wilderness Press).

The Hike Profile

Ⅰ SAMPLE PROFILE: Gillette Lake

SCENERY: ☆ ☆

CHILDREN: ☆ ☆ ☆ ☆

SOLITUDE: ☆ ☆

HIKING TIME: 2–3 hours

TRAIL CONDITION: ☆ ☆ ☆

DIFFICULTY: ☆

DISTANCE: 5 miles

GREEN TRAILS MAP: *Bonneville Dam 429*

OUTSTANDING FEATURES: Access point to Table Mountain, a good early-season hike close to Portland and Vancouver. Hood River, Oregon, just 20 minutes away, offers great grub at its many cafés, wineries, and brewpubs.

The cool shade of the forest canopy provides relief on a hot, sunny hike to Gillette Lake.

IN ADDITION TO A MAP, each hike contains a concise but informative narration of the route, from beginning to end. This descriptive text is enhanced with at-a-glance ratings and information, GPS-based trailhead coordinates, and accurate driving directions leading from a major road to a parking area convenient to the trailhead.

At the beginning of each hike profile is an at-a-glance box that gives you easy access to the following information: quality of scenery, condition of the trail(s), appropriateness for children, difficulty, level of solitude expected, hike distance, approximate hiking time, and outstanding highlights of the trip.

The first five categories are rated from one to five stars. In the example on the previous page, the star ratings indicate that the scenery is passable but not great, the trail condition is good (one star would mean the trail is muddy, rocky, overgrown, or otherwise compromised), the hike is accessible for able-bodied children (a one-star rating would denote that only the most gung-ho and physically fit children should go), the hike is easy (five stars would be strenuous), and you can expect to encounter people on the trail (you may well be elbowing your way up the trail on one-star hikes).

Hiking times assume an average pace of 2–3 miles per hour, with time built in for pauses at overlooks and brief rests. Overnight hiking times account for the effort of carrying a backpack.

Following the key info and star ratings is a brief description of the hike. A more detailed account follows, in which trail junctions, stream crossings, and trailside features are noted, along with their distance from the trailhead. Flip through the book, read the brief descriptions, and choose some hikes that appeal to you.

Weather

WHEN MOST PEOPLE THINK OF WASHINGTON STATE, the word *rain* usually comes to mind. The truth is, however, that Washington weather is actually quite varied. West of the Cascade Crest it's mild, with average temperatures ranging from the mid-70s in the summer to the mid-40s in the winter. The official rainy season begins in November and lasts through April. Weather east of the crest is marked by a much warmer summer, with average temperatures in the 90s. In the winter, snow levels drop to around 1,500 feet and temperatures dip into the low 20s. Occasionally, the difference in these two climates is dramatic, with bluebird skies in the east and a thick, dark wall of clouds hovering directly on the crest.

What does all this mean for the mountains in Washington? *Lots and lots of snow!* Some of the heaviest snowfall in the Lower 48 occurs on the PCT. While snow enthusiasts love this, avid hikers scurry from trailhead to trailhead to cram in as much hiking as possible before the snowflakes fly. To take full advantage of a hiking season in the Cascade Mountains, consider the pros and cons of where to go and when to head out.

MAY–JUNE: *Lasting Sunsets and Lingering Snow*

As the days in Washington get longer and warmer, many hikers itch with anticipation to hit the trails. While hiking in June is not uncommon, you should be prepared for an adventure: lingering snowfields, downed trees, washed-out bridges, and high-river crossings are just a few of the challenges you may encounter.

Before you head out, research trail conditions. If you discover that the high country is still snowbound, consider exploring the southern trails of the PCT, which lie at a lower elevation, or trails that run east of the crest, where the weather is a bit warmer and drier.

JULY–AUGUST: *Blooming Flowers and Buzzing Bugs*

These are by far the most popular months to hike. The weather is warm (although I got snowed on three times in August one summer), the meadows show off their vibrant array of wildflowers, and many of the alpine lakes are just getting warm enough to swim in. The only drawbacks are having to share the trails with other Pacific Northwest hikers and trying to escape the buzzing, biting insects that swarm the hillsides this time of year. Longer loop hikes into the alpine country are a great option during these hot summer months.

SEPTEMBER–OCTOBER: *Fall Delights and Frosty Nights*

Fall in the high country is a special time of year. Cold, crisp nights turn entire hillsides into a canvas of warm colors: the deep, rich reds of the huckleberry bush, the golden yellow of the larch. It's a quiet, peaceful time to be in the mountains but also a time during which you need to be prepared for below-freezing overnight temperatures and rapidly changing weather. Alternatively, take advantage of the numerous day hikes along the PCT.

Before any backcountry outing, check a detailed mountain weather forecast—if it doesn't say *sunny,* be prepared for anything. Also, while the public lands in this book are technically open year-round, many facilities, trails, and access roads in and around them close for the winter, so check with the resources in Appendix A, page 221, for the latest information.

Water

HOW MUCH IS ENOUGH? One simple physiological fact should convince you to err on the side of excess when deciding how much water to pack: A hiker working hard in 90° heat needs approximately 10 quarts of fluid per day. That's 2.5 gallons—12 large water bottles or 16 small ones. Pack along one or two bottles even for short hikes.

Some hikers and backpackers hit the trail prepared to purify water found along the route. This method, while less dangerous than drinking it untreated, comes with risks. Purifiers with ceramic filters are the safest. Many hikers pack along the slightly distasteful tetraglycine–hydroperiodide tablets to clean water (sold under the names Potable Aqua, Coughlan's, and so on).

Probably the most common waterborne bug that hikers ingest is giardia, which may not affect you until one to four weeks after you drink tainted water. (Let's just say that when it does hit, you'll know it.) Other parasites to worry about include *E. coli* and *Cryptosporidium,* both of which are harder to kill than giardia.

For most people, the pleasures of hiking make carrying water a relatively minor price to pay to remain healthy. If you're tempted to drink "found water," do so only if you understand the risks involved. Better yet, hydrate before your hike, carry (and drink) 6 ounces of water for every mile you plan to hike, and hydrate after the hike.

Alpine vistas abound along Nannie Ridge en route to Sheep Lake (see Hike 5, page 46).

Clothing

THE OUTDOOR-CLOTHING INDUSTRY has carved out a hot, trendy market, and trying to put an outfit together for a day in the backcountry can be downright mind-boggling. Fortunately, there are just a few things you need to keep in mind when figuring out how to stay warm, dry, and happy in the woods—how you *look* on the trail is entirely up to you.

Two basic kinds of materials are used in today's outdoor clothing: natural fibers and synthetics. Cotton, a natural fiber, is best left for the car ride home. When wet, it can even kill by absorbing moisture and robbing the body of heat. Wool, on the other hand, is an amazing natural fiber that insulates when dry, works when wet, and doesn't absorb odor nearly as easily as synthetic materials. If the thought of it makes you itchy, you haven't tried today's wool products, which are much softer than their predecessors.

The latest and most diverse materials used in today's outdoor clothing, synthetics range from those made of hollow fibers that trap air and heat to supertight weaves that allow vapor to pass through but resist water saturation.

Gore-Tex, soft shells, and polypropylenes are just a few of the names and words you'll see in discussions of synthetic clothing.

Because both synthetic and natural fibers work only as well as your ability to manage them, it's extremely important to layer properly. Make sure that you pack enough cool layers that you don't leave a trail of sweat when climbing to a pass and enough warm layers to enjoy an afternoon sunset from an alpine ridge.

Most important, be prepared for the full range of weather. Lightweight, breathable raingear is an essential piece of your layering system when it comes to hiking in the great Northwest. Even if it doesn't rain, a lightweight shell can block chilly wind, trap in heat, and be a lifesaver against swarms of bloodthirsty mosquitoes.

Equipment

KEEPING UP WITH THE LATEST AND GREATEST ultralight gizmos and gadgets is not my cup of tea. My husband, on the other hand, can spend hours researching gear before he even sets foot in a store. No matter where you land on the technology spectrum, a few essentials should accompany you on every outdoor adventure.

Footwear

This is the most important piece of equipment that you'll use on the trail. A 4-mile day hike can quickly turn into a blister-filled torture-fest if you don't have the right shoes for the job. Many shoe companies are now making low-top hiking shoes, which are a little stiffer, have beefier tread, and are more water-resistant than the typical running shoe. These shoes work great for long day hikes with a light pack.

If you need a little more support, try a lightweight hiking boot, which is a good option if you're hiking with a heavy pack, you have weak ankles, or you plan to explore off-trail. Regardless of the footwear you choose, make sure that you test it around town or on local trails before you head into the backcountry.

Backpack

If you're in the market for a new backpack, you're in luck. You have probably 100 different styles, colors, and sizes to choose from. Although the task may seem a little overwhelming, the number of options out there allows you to find a pack that meets your specific needs. A pack that fits well won't leave you standing in your living room debating whether or not you should save an ounce by leaving that extra chocolate bar at home. Spend a little more time and money to find a pack that works.

Essential Gear

Today you can buy outdoor vests that have up to 20 pockets shaped and sized to carry everything from toothpicks to binoculars. Or, if you don't aspire to feel like a burro, you can neatly stow all of these items in your day pack or backpack. The following list showcases never-hike-without-them items—in alphabetical order, as all are important:

EXTRA CLOTHES Raingear (for the occasional rainy day), a change of socks, and depending on the season, a warm hat and gloves

EXTRA FOOD Trail mix, granola bars, or other high-energy snacks

FLASHLIGHT OR HEADLAMP For getting back to the trailhead if you take longer than expected. Also bring along an extra bulb and batteries.

INSECT REPELLENT To ward off ticks and other biting bugs

MAPS AND A HIGH-QUALITY COMPASS GPS is great technology, but don't rely on it as your sole navigational tool.

POCKETKNIFE and/or multitool

SUN PROTECTION Sunglasses with UV tinting, a sunhat with a wide brim, and sunscreen

TOILET PAPER and a zip-top plastic bag to pack it out in

WATER Again, bring more than you think you'll drink. Depending on your destination, you may want to bring a container and iodine or a filter for purifying water in case you run out.

WHISTLE It could become your best friend in an emergency.

WINDPROOF MATCHES AND/OR A LIGHTER For real emergencies—please don't start a forest fire.

A Few Extras

Some items that might be worth the extra weight:

TREKKING POLES OR A HIKING STICK A great way to save your knees

REPAIR KIT Safety pins, duct tape, extra shoelaces, and the like

FLIP-FLOPS, SANDALS, OR CLOGS When you're hanging out at camp, casual shoes create less of an impact on fragile vegetation than heavy boots or hiking shoes—and nothing feels better than airing out your feet after a long day on the trail.

Shelter

For most people, tents are a necessity when it comes to backpacking in the Northwest. Not only do they keep you dry and warm in foul weather, they can also save you from mosquitoes and biting flies. July and August are about the only months in Washington when you can toy with the idea of leaving the tent at home. If you do, bring some type of emergency shelter or bivy sack and a bug net for hanging out and sleeping.

Even if you're just out for the day, bring some type of shelter to keep you out of the elements if something should go wrong. Building a shelter out of twigs and limbs may sound romantic, but in an emergency you want something that will keep you relatively warm and dry on the shortest notice. Emergency blankets weigh next to nothing and don't cost that much.

First Aid Kit

A TYPICAL FIRST AID KIT may contain more items than you might think necessary. These are just the basics. Prepackaged kits in waterproof bags (Atwater Carey and Adventure Medical make a variety of kits) are available. Even though there are quite a few items listed here, they pack down into a small space:

- Adhesive bandages
- Antibiotic ointment (such as Neosporin)
- Aspirin, acetaminophen (Tylenol), or ibuprofen (Advil)

This well-prepared crew hikes along Cady Ridge (see Hike 23, page 152).

- Athletic tape
- Blister kit (moleskin or an adhesive variety such as Spenco 2nd Skin)
- Butterfly-closure bandages
- Diphenhydramine (Benadryl), in case of allergic reactions
- Elastic bandages (such as Ace) or joint wraps (such as Spenco)
- Epinephrine in a prefilled syringe (EpiPen), typically by prescription only, for people known to have severe allergic reactions to hiking mishaps such as bee stings
- Gauze (one roll and a half-dozen 4-by-4-inch pads)
- Hydrogen peroxide or iodine

Hiking with Children

NO ONE IS TOO YOUNG FOR A HIKE. Be mindful, though. Flat, short, and shaded trails are best with an infant. Toddlers who haven't quite mastered walking can still tag along, riding on an adult's back in a child carrier. Use common sense to judge a child's capacity to hike a particular trail and always anticipate that the child will tire quickly and need to be carried. See Recommended Hikes, page xi, for hikes that are suitable for kids.

General Safety

TO SOME POTENTIAL MOUNTAIN ENTHUSIASTS, the deep woods seem inordinately dark and perilous. It's fear of the unknown that causes this anxiety. No doubt, potentially dangerous situations can occur outdoors, but as long as you use sound judgment and prepare yourself before hitting the trail, you'll be much safer in the woods than in most urban areas of the country. It's better to look at a backcountry hike as a fascinating chance to discover the unknown rather than as a chance for potential disaster.

If you're new to the game, I'd suggest starting out easy and finding a person who knows more to help you out. In addition, here are a few tips to make your trip safer and easier.

- **ALWAYS LET SOMEONE KNOW WHERE YOU'LL BE HIKING AND HOW LONG YOU EXPECT TO BE GONE.** It's a good idea to give that person a copy of your route, particularly if you're headed into any isolated area. Let him or her know when you return.

- **ALWAYS SIGN IN AND OUT OF ANY TRAIL REGISTERS PROVIDED.** Don't hesitate to comment on the trail condition if space is provided; that's your opportunity to alert others to any problems you encounter.

- **DON'T ASSUME THAT YOUR MOBILE PHONE WILL WORK ON THE TRAIL.** Reception may be spotty or nonexistent, especially on a trail embraced by towering trees.

- **ALWAYS CARRY FOOD AND WATER, EVEN FOR A SHORT HIKE.** And bring more water than you think you'll need. We can't emphasize this enough.

Signs warn hikers and horsepackers of precarious trail conditions below Old Snowy Mountain (see Hike 6, page 51).

■ **ASK QUESTIONS.** Public-land employees are on hand to help. It's a lot easier to solicit advice before a problem occurs, and it will help you avoid a mishap away from civilization when it's too late to amend an error.

■ **STAY ON DESIGNATED TRAILS.** Even on the most clearly marked trails, you usually reach a point where you have to stop and consider in which direction to head. If you become disoriented, don't panic. As soon as you think you may be off-track, stop, assess your current direction, and then retrace your steps to the point where you went astray. Using a map, a compass, and this book, and keeping in mind what you've passed thus far, reorient yourself and trust your judgment on which way to continue. If you become absolutely unsure of how to continue, return to your vehicle the way you came in. Should you become completely lost and have no idea how to find the trailhead, remaining in place along the trail and waiting for help is most often the best option for adults and always the best option for children.

- **ALWAYS CARRY A WHISTLE,** another precaution that we can't overemphasize. It may become a lifesaver if you get lost or hurt.

- **BE ESPECIALLY CAREFUL WHEN CROSSING STREAMS.** Whether you're fording the stream or crossing on a log, make every step count. If you have any doubt about maintaining your balance on a log, ford the stream instead: use a trekking pole or stout stick for balance and *face upstream as you cross.* If a stream seems too deep to ford, turn back. Whatever is on the other side isn't worth risking your life for.

- **BE CAREFUL AT OVERLOOKS.** While these areas may provide spectacular views, they are potentially hazardous. Stay back from the edge of outcrops, and make absolutely sure of your footing—a misstep can mean a nasty and possibly fatal fall.

- **STANDING DEAD TREES AND STORM-DAMAGED LIVING TREES POSE A SIGNIFICANT HAZARD TO HIKERS.** These trees may have loose or broken limbs that could fall at any time. While walking beneath trees, and when choosing a spot to rest or enjoy your snack, *look up.*

- **KNOW THE SYMPTOMS OF SUBNORMAL BODY TEMPERATURE, OR HYPOTHERMIA.** Shivering and forgetfulness are the two most common indicators of this stealthy killer. Hypothermia can occur at any elevation, even in the summer—especially if you're wearing lightweight cotton clothing. If symptoms develop, get to shelter, hot liquids, and dry clothes as soon as possible.

- **LIKEWISE, KNOW THE SYMPTOMS OF ABNORMALLY HIGH BODY TEMPERATURE, OR HYPERTHERMIA.** Here's how to recognize and handle three types of heat emergencies:

    Heat cramps in the legs and abdomen are accompanied by heavy sweating and feeling faint. Caused by excessive salt loss, these painful cramps must be handled by getting to a cool place and sipping water or an electrolyte solution (such as Gatorade).

    Dizziness, headache, irregular pulse, disorientation, and nausea are all symptoms of *heat exhaustion,* which occurs as blood vessels dilate and attempt to move heat from the inner body to the skin. Find a cool place, drink cool water, and get a friend to fan you, which can help cool you off more quickly.

    Heatstroke is a life-threatening condition that can cause convulsions, unconsciousness, and even death. If you should be sweating and you're not, that's the signature warning sign—your hike is over at this point. Other symptoms include dilated pupils; dry, hot, flushed skin; a rapid pulse; high fever; and abnormal breathing. If you or a hiking partner is experiencing heatstroke, do whatever you can to cool down and get help.

- **MOST IMPORTANTLY, TAKE ALONG YOUR BRAIN.** A cool, calculating mind is the single most important asset on the trail. Think before you act. Watch your step. Plan ahead. Avoiding accidents before they happen is the best way to ensure a rewarding and relaxing hike.

Animal, Plant, and Insect Hazards

THE FOLLOWING LIST is by no means intended to scare you off of heading into the mountains, but rather to inform you of potential hazards and advise you on ways to mitigate them. In all likelihood, the only bear or cougar you'll encounter is the one pictured on the information board, ticks will choose to hang out in the bushes, and beautiful sunsets will replace memories of biting mosquitoes.

Mosquitoes and Biting Flies

The peak of mosquito season in the Cascades is usually around July. As the snow melts, stagnant water and warm temperatures combine to create the perfect mosquito habitat. The best way to handle these pesky insects is to wear long sleeves, bring a tent with good ventilation, and, as a last resort, use some type of insect repellent.

Mosquitoes are capable of transmitting West Nile virus, which is most commonly spread from mosquitoes that have fed on an infected bird. The first case of the virus in the United States was reported in 1999, and it was not reported in Washington until 2006. Most people who carry the virus don't get sick. A few people report flulike symptoms and even fewer have severe reactions. If you find yourself feeling ill after being exposed to mosquitoes, see a doctor immediately.

Biting flies are another one of nature's nuisances. Horseflies and deer-flies are large, and their bite delivers a mighty punch that can itch for days. Midges, also known as no-see-ums, have a vicious, itchy bite out of proportion with their tiny size. Follow the same precautions as for mosquitoes.

Ticks

Blood-feeding parasites that are related to spiders, ticks can transmit Lyme disease and other illnesses. Cases of tick-related diseases are few in Washington State, but it's more than worth your time to take the necessary precautions, because extracting ticks from your skin is anything but fun.

The easiest way to avoid a tick bite is to wear a tightly woven long-sleeve shirt and light-colored pants so you can easily spot the tick's dark body on your clothing. Tuck your shirt into your pants and your pant legs inside your socks or boots, and if you're traveling in a tick-heavy area, consider using a tick repellent.

Lastly, make sure you do a thorough body check after hiking. When empty of blood, ticks are extremely hard to spot, so inspect yourself carefully, especially in warm, dark areas such as your armpits, groin, head, neck, and ears. Symptoms of tick-related illnesses resemble the flu, so see a doctor if you feel sick after hiking in tick country.

Bears

Two types of bears live in Washington State: the grizzly and the black. Black bears, the more common of the two, roam the Cascade Mountains. Grizzlies, on the other hand, are rare, and sightings of them even rarer. They are on Washington's endangered-species list, with reports estimating between 10 and 30 grizzly bears living in the northern part of the Cascades.

Most encounters with bears are brief, and you'll be lucky to catch a glimpse of their rumps waddling away as they run off toward safety. Remember: they're trying to avoid you just as much as you're trying to avoid them. To reduce your chance of an encounter, make plenty of noise when hiking, don't travel by yourself, hike with your dog on a leash (dogs may bring out defensive behaviors in bears), cook away from camp, and hang/securely store your food at night.

If you do have an encounter with a bear, try your best to remain calm, speak in a firm voice, and slowly back away. If you plan to travel in areas frequented by bears, particularly areas with grizzlies, you might consider carrying bear spray, which will more than likely remain in its case.

Cougars

If you should ever spot a cougar, feel honored. These big but timid cats work hard to remain unseen, and sightings of them are uncommon, especially in the wild. Nevertheless, you may encounter cougars that have accidentally stumbled into urban areas that are encroaching on their ever-shrinking habitat.

In the unlikely event that you encounter a cougar, remain calm. Speak to the cougar in an assertive voice, and try to make yourself look large and intimidating. Don't make any sudden movements, and keep your eyes on the animal at all times. If you have children with you, pick them up or move them close to you. If an attack ensues, *fight back.*

Rattlesnakes

The western rattlesnake prefers a warm, dry climate, such as is found on the eastern slopes of the Cascades. These rattlers hibernate during the winter in large numbers, tucking themselves into rock crevices on south-facing mountainsides, and slowly begin to emerge between March and May, dispersing to their summer habitats.

Like cougars, rattlesnakes are shy and prefer to hide from larger animals (including humans) to avoid being preyed on. Bites are extremely rare, and when they do occur, it's usually because someone was stupidly trying to capture or provoke the snake. If you hear a rattle, know that the snake is just alerting you that you're entering its territory.

Poisonous Edibles

Berries, mushrooms, and other edible plants thrive throughout Washington. These tasty natural treats are a true delight, but if you have even the slightest doubt about whether a plant is safe to eat, stick to your trail mix.

Poison Oak and Poison Ivy

These rash-producing plants are notorious for ruining a fun outing. Fortunately for those interested in exploring the PCT, poison oak and poison ivy have a difficult time growing above 4,000 feet. The downside to that upside: many PCT access trails begin at elevations much lower than this. Being aware of poison ivy and poison oak is key to having a safe, rash-free outing.

Poison oak has three oaklike leaflets, grows as a vine or shrub, and is the most common rash-producing plant in Washington. Poison ivy has three leaflets and can be a climbing or low-lying vine.

The body's reaction to the plants' oil, called urushiol, results in swelling, redness, blisters, and intense itching. Avoiding contact is the most effective way to avoid a rash. If you break out, resist the urge to scratch—dirty fingernails can cause sores to become infected. Oil-contaminated objects will continue to cause a reaction for at least a year, so thoroughly wash everything that may have urushiol on it, including clothing, boots, and pets.

Poison ivy

Poison oak

PHOTO: TOM WATSON

PHOTO: JANE HUBER

Tips for Enjoying the PCT in Washington

GIVE YOURSELF PLENTY OF TIME TO ENJOY AN AREA. Washington is a large state, and many of the trailheads along the PCT lie in remote areas. The last thing you want to do is spend an entire day in the car only to find that you have to practically run the trail to finish in time. Many of the hikes in a given region in this book leave from the same location or are a short drive from one another. Plan an extended weekend so you can truly enjoy these areas. I found that giving myself enough time allowed me to discover things I would have overlooked, from hidden alpine lakes to isolated back-country camps. Having a little extra time also lets you check out some of the small mountain towns scattered among the foothills of the PCT.

Ever heard the saying, "Slow and steady gets the turtle to the top?" It's a little mantra I learned from my high school cross-country coach, and it's one I find myself muttering when I have to climb a pass or hike a long distance. The tendency for many of us is to overexert ourselves by attempting to get a steep hill or series of switchbacks over with as quickly as possible. These sprints will force you to stop every 5 minutes to catch your breath and will leave you sweat-drenched by the time you reach your destination. To avoid overdoing it, pace yourself and enjoy your surroundings. For long climbs, plan a break every hour or so and hydrate and refuel each time you stop. When you do finally make it to the top, reward yourself with a "hill pill," such as a chunk of chocolate or a gooey piece of caramel.

As every Pacific Northwesterner knows, it's important to take advantage of good weather in Washington. Most of us, however, can't control our schedules, and it isn't surprising for our days off to coincide with a forecast that calls for "mostly to partly cloudy with a chance of showers." While not ideal, this kind of weather has its perks. The crowds are quieter, the hiking temperature is cooler, and there's nothing more beautiful than watching clouds pour over a jagged ridgeline at sunset. While it's not advisable to go out in a blizzard in June or a severe thunderstorm in July, a little drizzle shouldn't keep you indoors all weekend. Of course, if you do head out in less than ideal weather, plan accordingly by reading a detailed weather forecast and bringing along all the necessary clothing and equipment to do so safely.

Backcountry Advice

IF THERE'S JUST ONE PIECE OF ADVICE I can pass along to hikers, it's to plan ahead. Whether it's the first time you've set foot in a wilderness area or the 500th time, doing a little homework before you hit the trail will ensure you get the most out of your backcountry experience.

- ◼ **CHECK THE WEATHER BEFORE YOU LEAVE HOME.** Access, particularly in Washington, can be a nightmare come spring, when the snow begins to melt and the damage of winter is revealed. Throughout winter and spring, avalanches rip from mountainsides, knocking over large, old-growth trees as if they were matchsticks. Heavy spring rains and upper-elevation snowmelts flood rivers and create landslides, washing out vital sections of trails, roads, and bridges. Local forest and park-service ranger stations have a wealth of information on current conditions as well as on seasonal facility and road closures.

- ◼ **CAREFULLY REVIEW LAND-ACCESS REGULATIONS.** Once you know where you want to go, the next step is figuring out the rules and regulations that apply there. As you'll quickly learn, each agency differs in how it manages public lands. For example, you must have a Northwest Forest Pass to park at many U.S. Forest Service trailheads, and while Mount Rainier National Park generally charges an entrance fee, North Cascades National Park does not.

- ◼ **MAKE ARRANGEMENTS IN ADVANCE FOR BACKCOUNTRY CAMPING.** Permits and rules also vary among agencies. North Cascades National Park, Mount Rainier National Park, and the Alpine Lakes Wilderness Area require you to register and to camp only at designated sites. Dogs are not permitted on trails in national parks and in some wilderness areas.

  As you can see, remembering the rules and regulations can be challenging. To assist you in planning your trip, we provide a contact list for each hike in the back of this book.

- ◼ **TRAVEL AND CAMP ON DURABLE SURFACES.** To help minimize your impact on the land, please camp at designated sites wherever they're available. Otherwise, look for places that other hikers have clearly already used, and camp on sturdy surfaces such as grass, rock, dirt, or snow. Avoid camping and hiking in fragile alpine meadows.

- ◼ **DISPOSE OF WASTE PROPERLY.** Pack it in, pack it out. Take all trash, including toilet paper and hygiene products, with you when you go. Bury human waste at least 200 feet from water sources, camps, and trails in a cathole 6–8 inches deep. Cover your cathole with plenty of dirt, and disguise it with needles and leaves when your business is finished.

- **MINIMIZE CAMPFIRE IMPACTS.** Campfires, particularly in the backcountry, are unnecessary these days, especially with the wide assortment of lightweight stoves available for cooking. If you do decide to build a fire, know the restrictions for the area you're visiting. Fires are often prohibited near lakes, in high-use areas or alpine zones, or whenever bans are in effect.

Trail Etiquette

WHEN IT COMES TO BEING CONSIDERATE on the trail, keep in mind that it's the small stuff that counts. While you may not initially see the problem with trampling a lupine or feeding a chipmunk, over time these actions have significant detrimental effects on the environment. The following tips describe just a few ways you can help ensure that future generations will continue to enjoy the wildness of the wilderness.

- **APPRECIATE WILDLIFE FROM A DISTANCE.** If you're fortunate enough to see wildlife, try to avoid spooking or startling it by quietly observing from a safe distance. Keep your food away from animals by storing it securely and making sure no scraps are left behind. Camp at least 200 feet from water sources so that wildlife have constant access to drinking water.

- **BE CONSIDERATE OF THOSE AROUND YOU.** Most hikers are looking to get away from the hustle and bustle of everyday life—respect their wishes by giving them plenty of space and keeping loud noises to a minimum. Also, try to leave an area in its natural state so that others may enjoy it.

- **TREAD LIGHTLY.** Stay on existing trails whenever possible, especially near lakes or campsites. Avoid blazing new paths, further contributing to the maze of social trails (nondesignated trails that hikers create over time to access water, check out a viewpoint, get to a campsite, and so on) in these areas. A lot of hard work and money went into creating these amazing trails, so do your part by respecting closures or areas that are being restored.

- **DON'T PICK THE FLOWERS.** Wildflowers, particularly those in alpine environments, have a very short growing season and are therefore easily destroyed. *Please* don't eat or walk, camp, rest, kneel, or nap on these fragile gems.

South: Oregon Border to White Pass

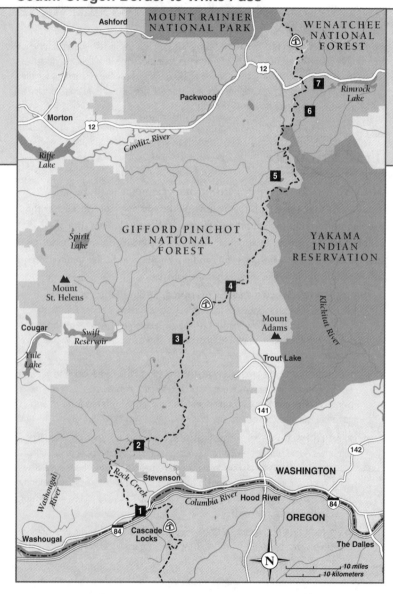

PART I: SOUTH

Oregon Border to White Pass

Spring flowers line the banks of Gillette Lake (see next page).

1 Gillette Lake

SCENERY: ✿ ✿   TRAIL CONDITION: ✿ ✿ ✿

CHILDREN: ✿ ✿ ✿ ✿   DIFFICULTY: ✿

SOLITUDE: ✿ ✿   DISTANCE: 5 miles

HIKING TIME: 2–3 hours   GREEN TRAILS MAP: *Bonneville Dam 429*

OUTSTANDING FEATURES: Access point to Table Mountain, a good early-
season hike close to Portland and Vancouver. Hood River, Oregon, just 20 minutes
away, offers great grub at its many cafés, wineries, and brewpubs.

ALTHOUGH NOT THE MOST AESTHETIC hike that runs along the Pacific
Crest Trail (PCT) in Washington, this is one of the first to melt out in the
spring, and its proximity to Portland and Vancouver makes it an easy half-day
getaway. This trail is also the access point for Table Mountain, one of the more
prominent features on the Washington side of the Columbia River Gorge.

🚶🚶   This hike can begin a couple of ways. Those interested in hiking on the
PCT the entire time can begin from a small parking pulloff just south of the
Bridge of the Gods on WA 14 (look for the large PACIFIC CREST TRAIL sign).
This option adds 1.4 miles to the overall hike and begins on an old, somewhat
overgrown power line road that parallels the highway. In a little less than a
mile, the trail works its way up a couple of switchbacks before joining Tamanous Trail, your second option for beginning this hike.

Tamanous Trail is the standard approach for Gillette Lake and begins
from the well-established Bonneville Trailhead, as shown on the map on page
26. The hike leaves from the far end of the lot, making a leisurely ascent on
a well-trodden trail. In less than 0.25 mile, you get a nice view of the Columbia River. A short distance on, the trail turns north and gains a small ridge,
where an abandoned clear-cut offers open views to the northwest.

A half mile from the trailhead, the path intersects the PCT. From this
junction, head north. Approximately 0.1 mile on, you should see a small
pond tucked in a stand of trees when you look downslope. These ponds, scattered throughout the area, are easy to miss if you aren't paying attention.

The next mile is a mixture of clear-cuts and forests—a good reminder of what the majority of this area would look like if numerous conservation groups had not worked hard to preserve much of the land around the Columbia Gorge. As you meander along, you might also notice that there's a mix of public and private land through this section. The property owners have allowed access, so please be respectful and stay on the main trail.

In 1.3 miles, the trail enters a thick forest that offers welcome shade on a hot summer day. As you stroll along, take note of the fern-covered knolls and large mossy boulders, remnants of a massive landslide that tore down the southern slopes of Table Mountain between 250 and 900 years ago. The slide traveled more than 5.5 miles on its journey to the Columbia River, where it created a 200-foot-high earthen dam. Native Americans referred to the site as "Bridge of the Gods."

In less than 1 mile, the trail climbs slightly before popping you out on a utility road that serves three sets of Bonneville Dam power lines. Try to ignore the loud buzzing noise because the view from here isn't too shabby. Table Mountain's scarred south face looms in the distance, helping you appreciate how big the Bonneville Landslide actually was.

Pick up the trail to Gillette Lake on the far side of the service road, where you can glimpse the lake's blue-green waters. Continue downhill; just before you reach the lake's seasonal inlet, a spur trail branches off to the left, to a nice shoreline lunch spot. If the lake is busy, you'll find a couple more good break spots as you head upstream along the inlet.

Although the lake is modest in size, it's a tranquil place to spend an afternoon fishing (the lake is stocked with golden trout), swimming, reading, or just relaxing. Once you're rejuvenated, simply retrace your steps to the trailhead.

For those of you looking for something slightly more ambitious, you can continue up the PCT to West Table Mountain Trail. Be prepared for a long, strenuous day. Table Mountain Trail is 15.8 miles round-trip and gains 3,350 feet, mostly in the last few miles.

If you find yourself with a couple hours to kill but don't quite have the energy to climb Table Mountain, consider taking a self-guided or ranger-led

Gillette Lake

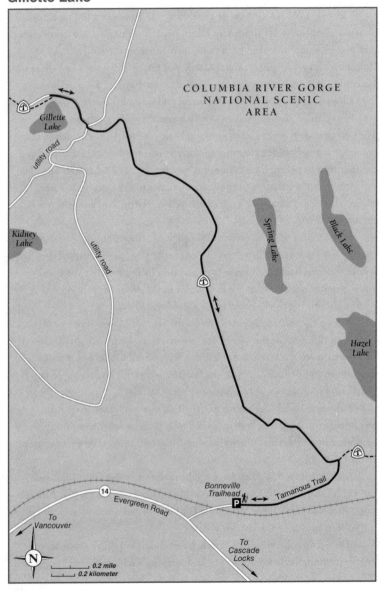

COLUMBIA RIVER GORGE
NATIONAL SCENIC
AREA

Gillette
Lake

utility road

Kidney
Lake

utility road

Spring Lake

Black Lake

Hazel
Lake

Bonneville
Trailhead

Tamanous Trail

14

Evergreen Road

P

To
Vancouver

To
Cascade
Locks

N

0.2 mile
0.2 kilometer

tour of Bonneville Dam, built in 1938 by the U.S. Army Corps of Engineers and still managed by them. There are visitor centers on the Washington and Oregon sides of the dam. For more information, call 541-374-8820.

PERMIT INFORMATION Northwest Forest Pass ($30/year) required; see tinyurl.com/northwestforestpass for more information.

DIRECTIONS

FROM PORTLAND: From I-84 just east of I-205, head east 40 miles to Cascade Locks. Take Exit 44 and keep right at the exit to reach the toll booth for Bridge of the Gods. Pay the toll and cross the Columbia River into Washington. Turn left (south, then west) onto WA 14 and drive 2 miles to the well-developed Bonneville Trailhead parking lot, on the right side of the road. *Note:* You'll pass the PCT trailhead pull-off just after you cross the Bridge of the Gods.

FROM VANCOUVER: Head east about 33 miles on WA 14 just east of I-205. After you go through the town of North Bonneville, keep an eye out for the Bonneville Dam, on your right. Just past the dam is the Bonneville Trailhead parking lot, on the left side of the road.

GPS TRAILHEAD COORDINATES N45° 39.110' W121° 55.888'

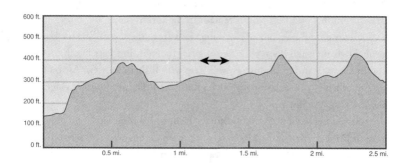

2 Bunker Hill

SCENERY: ✿	TRAIL CONDITION: ✿ ✿ ✿ ✿
CHILDREN: ✿ ✿	DIFFICULTY: ✿ ✿ ✿
SOLITUDE: ✿ ✿ ✿ ✿	DISTANCE: 3.6 miles
HIKING TIME: 2–3 hours	GREEN TRAILS MAP: *Wind River 397*

OUTSTANDING FEATURES: Old-growth Douglas-fir trees, a historical interpretive trail, and a chance to stand atop an old volcanic plug

IF YOU'RE LIKE ME, you find spring in the Pacific Northwest an antsy time of year. While you patiently wait for the upper-elevation hikes to melt out, consider burning some energy with an early-season leg burner to the top of Bunker Hill. This steady climb gains 1,200 feet in less than 1.5 miles along a series of switchbacks that zigzags its way up the hillside. Views from the top are limited, but the feeling of accomplishment makes it worth the effort.

🚶🚶 To begin this hike, head north on the Pacific Crest Trail (PCT) through a large meadow bursting with daffodils and dandelions in late spring. As you traverse the meadow, note the large, forested mound ahead. This is Bunker Hill, an igneous volcanic plug that was pushed up through layers of lava flows and volcanic debris 20–25 million years ago.

Continue through the meadow, and in less than 0.25 mile the trail enters a stand of deciduous trees whose leaves rustle even in the lightest of breezes. In another 0.25 mile, the trail reaches the signed turnoff for Bunker Hill. From this point on, you'll remain in the forest.

Older guidebooks talk of sweeping views from the top of Bunker Hill, probably from when it was still used as a fire lookout, but I ate lunch on the top in a thick stand of second-growth trees with little to no view. As you hike up the hillside, you occasionally catch glimpses of the surrounding ridgelines, but the views are limited.

As you begin your climb up Bunker Hill, you'll soon see large, old-growth Douglas-fir and hemlock trees scattered throughout this second-growth forest. The Douglas-fir, in particular, played an important role

A flowering meadow at the base of Bunker Hill

in the history of this area and the way in which the United States manages forests today. The Wind River area is just one of 77 experimental forests in the United States. The Wind River branch was established in 1932; however, Thornton T. Munger, who later became the first director of the Pacific Northwest Research Station, began to conduct the relevant research for the U.S. Forest Service back in 1909.

This forest was originally used to study the great Douglas-fir forests of the Pacific Northwest, and many of the practices for studying, cultivating, and managing forests were developed during this period. Today the research facility is used primarily to study the ecosystem of Douglas-fir forests and research old-growth tree and wildlife habitats.

Bunker Hill

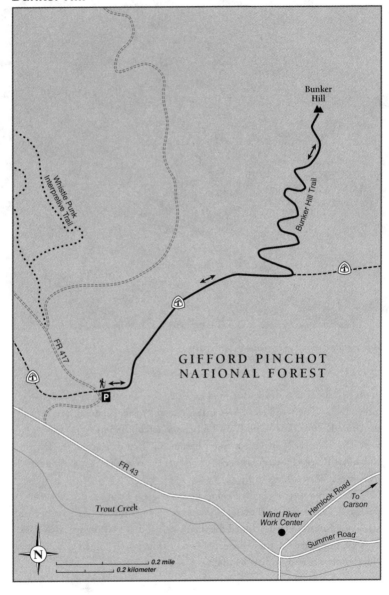

Bunker Hill

Bunker Hill Trail

Whistle Punk Interpretive Trail

FR 417

P

GIFFORD PINCHOT
NATIONAL FOREST

FR 43

Trout Creek

Wind River Work Center

Hemlock Road

To Carson

Summer Road

N

0.2 mile
0.2 kilometer

Continuing your climb, you'll notice that the first few switchbacks are relatively long and gradual. In less than 1 mile, the switchbacks tighten up and become a bit steeper as you inch closer to the summit. When you reach the last switchback, at 1.7 miles, you'll notice a path that branches off to the right, your only chance to see open views of the Wind River valley. Be careful: getting to this viewpoint is tricky, and a slip could be fatal. The U.S. Forest Service strongly encourages folks to stay on the main trail.

As you hike beyond the viewpoint, the trail makes one last, steep push to the top before reaching the summit of Bunker Hill (2,383'). The big clue that you've reached your final destination is the remnants of an abandoned U.S. Forest Service fire lookout. A few remaining foundation blocks make for a nice place to sit and have lunch. Once you've recovered from your ascent, simply retrace your footsteps the 1.8 miles to the start of the hike.

If you find yourself with a little extra time when you arrive back at the trailhead, check out Whistle Punk Interpretive Trail. To get there, walk 0.25 mile up Forest Road 417 to the trailhead parking area, on the right side of the road. The trail itself travels along a railroad grade that dates to 1913. Informative signs and a brochure tell the story of the Wind River Logging Company and the forest management practices associated with railroad logging. The trail also wanders through an old-growth forest, an old Wind River Nursery field, and past a wetland area. Choose between the 0.75- or the 1.5-mile loop.

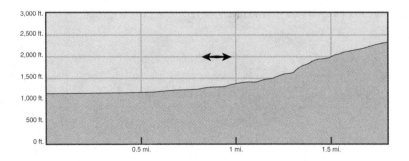

PERMIT INFORMATION Northwest Forest Pass ($30/year) required. See tinyurl.com/northwestforestpass for more information.

DIRECTIONS

FROM PORTLAND: From I-84 just east of I-205, head east 40 miles on I-84 to Cascade Locks. Take Exit 44 and keep right at the exit to reach the toll booth for Bridge of the Gods. Pay the toll and cross the Columbia River into Washington. Once over the bridge, turn right (north, then east) onto WA 14 and follow it 5.8 miles to the Carson exit.

FROM VANCOUVER: Drive east about 41 miles on WA 14 just east of I-205 to the Carson exit.

FROM WA 14: From the Carson exit, continue north 14.3 miles on Wind River Highway to Hemlock Road (you'll see a sign for the Wind River Work Center). Turn left on Hemlock and continue 1.5 miles to FR 43—this road, which is just to the right of the Wind River Work Center, is easy to miss if you aren't paying attention. Turn right onto FR 43 and drive 0.5 mile to FR 417. Turn right onto FR 417 and, just as you crest the hill, keep an eye out for the southbound PCT, on the left side of the road about 100 yards from the turnoff. Continue driving, and when the road makes a somewhat sharp turn to the left, you'll see the trailhead for the northbound PCT on the right side of the road.

GPS TRAILHEAD COORDINATES N45° 48.455' W121° 56.417'

3 Lemei Lake

SCENERY: ✿ ✿ ✿ ✿	TRAIL CONDITION: ✿ ✿ ✿ ✿
CHILDREN: ✿ ✿ ✿ ✿	DIFFICULTY: ✿ ✿ ✿
SOLITUDE: ✿ ✿ ✿	DISTANCE: 12.5 miles

HIKING TIME: 6–7 hours or overnight

GREEN TRAILS MAP: *Indian Heaven 365S*

OUTSTANDING FEATURES: Grassy meadows to lounge around in, endless fields of huckleberries, multiple lakes to laze away the afternoon, and a variety of hiking options

PANORAMIC VIEWS, WIDE-OPEN FIELDS, and a chance to stand on top of something are usually among my requirements for a good hike. So, when I stumbled across the Indian Heaven Wilderness, I have to admit I was skeptical; how interesting could a series of lakes through the woods really be? But this impressive scenery will keep the most extreme of alpine enthusiasts mesmerized. This hike is best done late summer or early fall, when the berries are ripe, the fields are bursting with color, and the mosquitoes are minimal.

One of the many quiet meadows along the Lemei Lake Loop

Lemei Lake

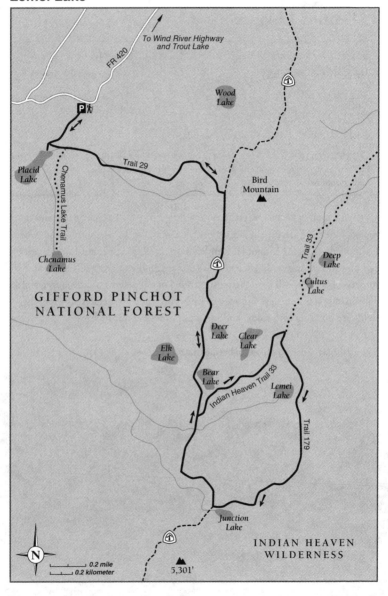

To Wind River Highway
and Trout Lake

FR 420

Wood
Lake

Placid
Lake

Chenamus Lake Trail

Trail 29

Bird
Mountain

Trail 33

Deep
Lake

Chenamus
Lake

Cultus
Lake

GIFFORD PINCHOT
NATIONAL FOREST

Deer
Lake

Clear
Lake

Elk
Lake

Bear
Lake

Indian Heaven Trail 33

Lemei
Lake

Trail 179

Junction
Lake

INDIAN HEAVEN
WILDERNESS

N

0.2 mile
0.2 kilometer

5,301'

👫   From the pullout, head south (across the road) to the trailhead, which is well established and easy to find. The trail is flat at the start and almost immediately enters the Indian Heaven Wilderness, an area rich in natural resources. Abundant berries, wild game, and fish have brought a number of American Indian tribes to this area for nearly 10,000 years. Many Indians continue to uphold their traditions in the Sawtooth Huckleberry Fields, which are some of the most productive huckleberry fields in the Northwest. Situated just east of Forest Road 24, parts of the fields are designated for exclusive use by the Yakama Nation through a handshake agreement with the U.S. Forest Service in 1932. As you'll probably notice on the hike to Placid Lake, many of the berries here are harvested as well. Not to worry, the entire hike is laden with a variety of huckleberry bushes, providing ample opportunities to sample one of nature's greatest treats.

After a pleasant 0.5-mile stroll through a large stand of timber, you reach the shallow waters of Placid Lake. The gentle descent is a good warm-up for the 1,000-foot climb from the lake up to the Pacific Crest Trail (PCT). Continue along the trail as it skirts just up from the southern shore of the lake, and in a short distance you reach a marked junction. Veer left, as the marker indicates, along Trail 29. The path quickly climbs above the lake, and in less than 0.5 mile, you reach the junction for Chenamus Lake (Trail 29A). Continue heading east on Trail 29.

From the junction, the trail makes a steady climb through a beautiful forest, alive with an assortment of mushrooms, moss-covered trees, and small

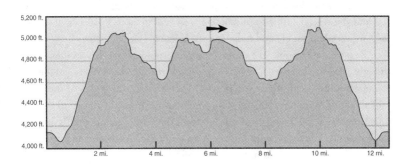

A striking view of Mount St. Helens

flowers. At 1.5 miles, the trail reaches a bench that rises above Placid Lake's inlet. By midsummer, the inlet looks more like a small meadow than a flowing creek. In another 0.3 mile, the trail passes a group of moss-covered boulders that mark the outlet of a tiny, unnamed pond, one of many in this area. Then it wraps around the pond and drops into a shrubby meadow. A few hundred more feet and you reach a lush grass meadow, a great spot to take a break late in summer or fall, when the ground is dry and the bugs are gone.

Beyond the meadow, the trail continues east-northeast. Just as the thought "Are we there yet?" begins to cross your mind, the trail crosses the top of a boulder field, where you're rewarded with a stunning view of the ashy flanks of Mount St. Helens. Take a moment to enjoy the image, as it's the only time you'll see the mystical volcano from the trail. From here, it's only a short distance before the trail tops out on a ridge, crossing an open meadow that offers views of Bird Mountain's forested slopes.

From the meadow, the trail reenters the woods and heads southeastward before reaching the PCT at 2.5 miles. Head south and soon reach a small boulder field with a series of murky ponds tucked among tall, green grass to the west of the trail. The trail is somewhat humdrum for the next mile or so. A sign marking the distance to Blue Lake, a popular destination for day and overnight hikers, is about the only significant landmark until you reach the junction for Clear Lake, where you head east, up Indian Heaven Trail 33.

The trail ascends steeply; however, the lake is not far, and the path quickly levels out. At first glance, Clear Lake seems like a clear version of a small pond, but as the trail works its way toward the northern shoreline, the lake's long southern shores are slowly revealed. Continuing on, the trail reaches a junction at 4.1 miles. Head south on Lemei Lake Trail 179. Trail 33 goes north to Cultus Lake and on to Cultus Creek Campground, a popular access point for this area.

I have to admit that this is my favorite part of the hike. While the PCT ambles through the forest, Lemei Lake Trail travels through vast open meadows full of low-lying huckleberry bushes. The chocolate-colored outlet of Lemei Lake is 1.5 miles from the junction with Clear Lake. From this point, you can enjoy views of Lemei Peak. As you approach the lake, you'll notice that the open terrain, abundant berries, and lack of people combine to create the perfect opportunity to see wildlife, which also makes it a great destination for an overnight. A small knoll above the lake, with plenty of tall trees for hanging food far from greedy paws, makes for a good spot to pitch a tent.

For those continuing on, follow the trail as it makes three steep switchbacks up and out of the Lemei Lake basin. The trail plateaus for a mile and wanders through more spectacular terrain. At 6.3 miles, the trail reenters the forest and makes a steep, somewhat rugged descent down to the pleasant waters of Junction Lake. You'll find a good campsite on the southwest shore and a decent one along the northwest shore.

Junction Lake is a fitting name—the junction with the PCT is on the eastern shoreline. Continue north on the PCT, and in 0.5 mile, you cross the dry bed of Lemei Creek. Notice the colorful pumice rocks in the streambed, a sign of the area's previous volcanic activity. As you amble through the woods, keep an eye out to the west for the muddy waters of Acker Lake, which is 1 mile or so from the junction. The trail crosses a couple of smaller, dried-up creeks and makes a gradual ascent as it approaches the bluish-green waters of Bear Lake, a popular destination for swimmers, loungers, day hikers, and backpackers. A junction with Elk Lake Trail 176 above the southeast corner of Bear Lake is a good place to access a couple of campsites on the lake's southwest shore.

Take a break at the lake, then continue north on the PCT. In 0.5 mile, the trail rounds the east side of Deer Lake, a smaller lake with less ideal camping than that at Bear. Just past the shoreline, you'll rejoin Indian Heaven Trail 33. From here, it's 3.5 miles back to the trailhead.

PERMIT INFORMATION Northwest Forest Pass ($30/year) required; see tinyurl.com/northwestforestpass for more information. Self-issued permits available at the trailhead.

DIRECTIONS To navigate this confusing area, stop by the Mount Adams Ranger Station in Trout Lake (2455 WA 141; 509-395-3402) to get a Mount St. Helens vicinity map. It doesn't show the many U.S. Forest Service roads, but it will give you an overall view of the area.

FROM PORTLAND: From I-84 in Portland just east of I-205, head east 56 miles to Hood River. Take Exit 64 and turn left (north) to cross the Columbia River into Washington on the Hood River Bridge. Once across the river, take the first left onto WA 14 and drive 1.5 miles; then turn right (north) onto WA 141 and drive 21 miles to the town of Trout Lake. Turn left at the fork to continue west on WA 141, passing the Mount Adams Ranger Station on your left in about a mile. Drive another mile and turn right (north) onto FR 88—from here, it's easiest to follow the signs for Mount St. Helens. Drive 13 miles until you reach four-way Big Tire Junction—you'll know when you're there. Veer left onto FR 8851, which becomes FR 24 in 5.5 miles. In another 1.1 miles, turn right onto FR 30, which is paved for the first 2.5 miles and then becomes gravel. Continue another 5.5 miles and turn left onto FR 420, which was unmarked at the time of this hike.

FROM SEATTLE: Take I-5 south from I-90 for 146 miles to Exit 21. Continue east on WA 503 for 46.7 miles; then turn right on FR 90, crossing Swift Reservoir and following the signs for Trout Lake. Continue 4.2 miles to the turnoff for Curly Creek Road, and turn right again. After 5.1 miles, turn left at the T onto Meadow Creek Road and continue about 3 miles. Veer right onto gravel FR 30. Continue about 2 miles and turn right onto FR 420, which was unmarked at this writing—if you reach milepost 38, you've gone too far.

ONCE ON FR 420: Continue 1 mile along FR 420. At this writing, the road was washed out 0.25 mile from the trailhead. While some brave souls may venture on in four-wheel-drive vehicles, it's just as easy to park on the shoulder and walk to the trailhead, on your right.

GPS TRAILHEAD COORDINATES N46° 2.915' W121° 48.550'

Tranquil waters flow out of Lemei Lake.

4 Horseshoe Meadow

SCENERY: ✿ ✿ ✿	TRAIL CONDITION: ✿ ✿ ✿ ✿ ✿
CHILDREN: ✿ ✿	DIFFICULTY: ✿ ✿ ✿
SOLITUDE: ✿ ✿ ✿	DISTANCE: 10 miles

HIKING TIME: 5 hours or overnight

GREEN TRAILS MAP: *Mount Adams 367S*

OUTSTANDING FEATURES: Up-close views of Mount Adams, large grassy meadows to lounge around in, and good huckleberry picking in August

AT 12,276 FEET, MOUNT ADAMS is the second-highest mountain in Washington and the third-highest in the Cascade Range. Yet most Northwesterners have never even been to this amazing wilderness area. Mount Adams is easily overshadowed by its popular neighbors, Mount Rainier National Park and Mount St. Helens National Volcanic Monument. If you want to escape the crowds on a long weekend, check out this often-overlooked Washington gem.

🚶🚶 I am a huge fan of small mountain communities in recreational Meccas. Therefore, cute, outdoorsy Trout Lake, near this hike's trailhead, shouldn't have surprised me. Surrounded by miles upon miles of trails and tucked beneath the graceful silhouette of Mount Adams, this little mountain town should be on your list of cool places to visit. Oh yeah, there's lots of great hiking, too.

Once you make it to the trailhead, head north along the Pacific Crest Trail (PCT) and, in 0.25 mile, reach a campsite near a permanent creek. Because there's no water late in the summer elsewhere in this area, you may see PCT thru-hikers and backpackers camped out at this spot. Continue across the bridge and, in another 0.25 mile, reach the Mount Adams Wilderness boundary. The next mile or so is pleasant as the trail winds through the forest, crossing a couple of creeks that can be dry by late summer.

At 1.7 miles, the trail makes a short, steep ascent that will make you appreciate the warm-up you've been enjoying up to this point. After a few hundred feet, the trail levels off and heads eastward through an open stand where waist-high huckleberry bushes cover the forest floor. At approximately 2.5 miles, the trail descends slightly as it crosses the usually dry White Salmon River, more of a small stream. Just before the trail switchbacks (approximately 100 yards from the crossing) a spring 50 yards below the trail is a good source for water.

Once you round the switchback, the trail turns north and the forest becomes thick as you cross the indiscernible river again. At 3.2 miles, the trail makes another turn to the east, and in 0.3 mile, it passes an overhanging boulder that would barely shelter one small person. This boulder also marks the entry into the subalpine, where low-lying huckleberry bushes interlaced with bunches of lupine cover the ground.

The trail descends gradually through small meadows and stands of Douglas-fir and mountain hemlock. At 4.2 miles, cross a small boulder with a flat top, a great spot for appreciating your first good view of Mount Adams, perfectly framed. You can't help but wonder if the boulder was intentionally placed.

Mount Adams's White Salmon Glacier dominates the landscape as you enter Horseshoe Meadow.

Horseshoe Meadow

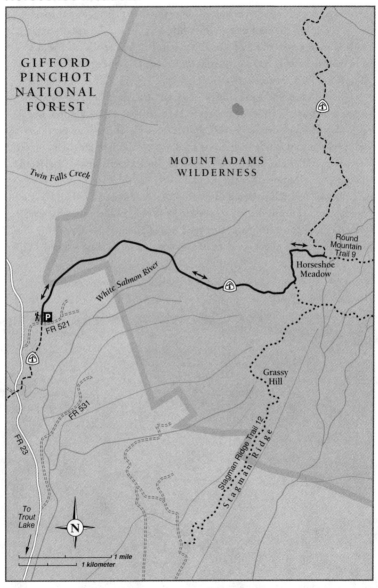

GIFFORD
PINCHOT
NATIONAL
FOREST

Twin Falls Creek

MOUNT ADAMS
WILDERNESS

White Salmon River

FR 521

FR 531

FR 23

To
Trout
Lake

N

Round
Mountain
Trail 9

Horseshoe
Meadow

Grassy
Hill

Stagman Ridge Trail 12

S t a g m a n   R i d g e

1 mile

1 kilometer

Just past this spot is an eye-catching meadow with a large rock outcropping that looks as if one side of it was hit with a gigantic hammer and broken into hundreds of pieces. Logs have been placed in the trail that leads into the meadow to keep people from trampling this fragile area. Not to worry—there are plenty of other good places, with heartier vegetation and more spectacular scenery, to take a break.

As the trail rounds the meadow, it eventually passes another jumble of boulders that has been overrun with huckleberry bushes, which seem to grow out of every crack and crevice. At 4.7 miles, the trail intersects Stagman Ridge Trail 12, which heads south toward Forest Road 120.

Continue east along the PCT and, in 0.25 mile, reach another junction with Round Mountain Trail 9. If you head southeast along this trail, past the unmarked wooden post with the carved tip, you'll soon arrive at Dry Lake Camp. (Noting the name, pack in water if you're interested in camping here.) Views of both the mountain and Horseshoe Meadow are excellent from this location.

If you have energy to burn, you can add a nice 4.3-mile loop to your hike by following Trail 9 east to where it joins Trail 9A. Follow it downhill to Looking Glass Lake, a quaint lake nestled in the trees with a view of Mount Adams from the southwest shore. Finish the loop by continuing northwest to the junction with the PCT.

For those interested in exploring the PCT from the junction, the trail makes a sharp bend as it skirts the meadow where Mount Adams's

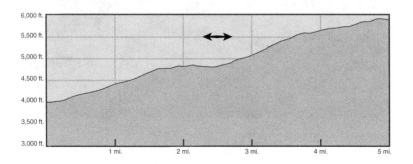

A closer view of Mount Adams's White Salmon Glacier

White Salmon Glacier can be seen clinging to the crumbly pumice slopes that seem to be holding the mountain together. The view disappears as the trail begins a short climb to the northwest. As the trail follows the west side of the ridge, you can see Mount Rainier to the northwest, which makes the extra elevation gain worth the effort. A series of large, flat boulders, 0.7 mile from the junction, marks a nice alpine setting to have lunch and call it a day. If you feel overly motivated or want to do an out-and-back overnight trip, continue another 3 miles to reach the shallow, murky waters of Sheep Lake.

PERMIT INFORMATION Northwest Forest Pass ($30/year) required; see tinyurl.com/northwestforestpass for more information. Self-issued permits available at the trailhead.

DIRECTIONS From I-84 in Portland just east of I-205, head east 56 miles to Hood River. Take Exit 64 and turn left (north) to cross the Columbia River into Washington on the Hood River Bridge. Once across the river, take the first left onto WA 14 and drive 1.5 miles; then turn right (north) onto WA 141. After 21 miles, the road forks—where WA 141 heads west into the town of Trout Lake, continue north on Mount Adams Road across the White Salmon River. In another 1.3 miles, the road splits again—take the left fork onto Forest Road 23, and follow it 13 miles north until you see a sign for the PCT on the left side of the road. Turn right onto Forest Road 521 and, after about 0.5 mile, park in the pullout on the left side of the road.

GPS TRAILHEAD COORDINATES N46° 10.241' W121° 37.590'

5 Nannie Ridge

SCENERY: ✿ ✿ ✿ ✿	TRAIL CONDITION: ✿ ✿ ✿ ✿
CHILDREN: ✿ ✿	DIFFICULTY: ✿ ✿ ✿
SOLITUDE: ✿ ✿ ✿	DISTANCE: 14.5 miles
HIKING TIME: 1–2 days	GREEN TRAILS MAP: *Walupt Lake 335*

OUTSTANDING FEATURES: A small alpine lake surrounded by fields of wildflowers, with fabulous views of the Goat Rocks and Mount Adams; a loop hike through scenic high country; and lots of great swimming holes to cool off in

IF YOU WANT TO EXPLORE the Goat Rocks Wilderness but don't have time to make it all the way into the heart of the mountains, check out the sweeping views from the flowery meadows along Nannie Ridge. Depending on where you live, the drive to Walupt Creek Campground can be long, so make a weekend of it by car camping and completing the loop as a long day hike—or better yet, spend a night in the high country.

A word of caution: if you visit this area in the fall, make sure that you and your four-legged companion wear bright colors—this area is popular with hunters.

From the northwest corner of Walupt Lake (3,930'), follow the painted horseshoes (a sign of this area's popularity with horsepackers) to the trailhead for Walupt Creek Trail 101. You'll reach Nannie Ridge Trail 98 within the first few hundred feet—take it, and slowly and steadily climb 2,000 feet.

The first 1.5 miles of the hike are unremarkable. The trail travels through thick, forested slopes with little to no views up a north-trending path. At 1.7 miles, the forest slowly begins to open as you continue your ascent into the high country, and for the first time you can see the stubby profile of Mount St. Helens to the southwest.

After a series of switchbacks, at 2.5 miles the trail tops out on a spur ridge that comes off the south side of Nannie Peak. If you're looking for a short excursion, you'll find great views by hiking 0.5 mile along an abandoned trail to the 6,106-foot summit of Nannie Peak. The trail is obvious and heads north from the ridge.

Continuing with the loop, follow Nannie Ridge Trail as it makes a slight descent, bypassing a cliff band that heads east off Nannie Peak. The craggy cliffs are impressive, and their color contrasts nicely with that of the fields of blooming flowers at their base.

Reach a small pond with a couple of campsites at 3.3 miles. The views from here aren't nearly as stunning as they are from Sheep Lake, but if you want more solitude or a short overnight excursion, this is not a bad option.

Leaving the pond, the trail begins a slight ascent through open slopes to a grassy saddle and the perfect place for an afternoon lunch. Views from here are fantastic, with the glaciated, gleaming slopes of Mount Adams to the south and the dry, arid mountains of the Goat Rocks Wilderness to the north. From here, the trail pleasantly rolls along Nannie Ridge and, at 4.5 miles, arrives at the quaint Sheep Lake (5,710'), whose tranquil green-blue waters and

A gorgeous summer day at Sheep Lake

Nannie Ridge

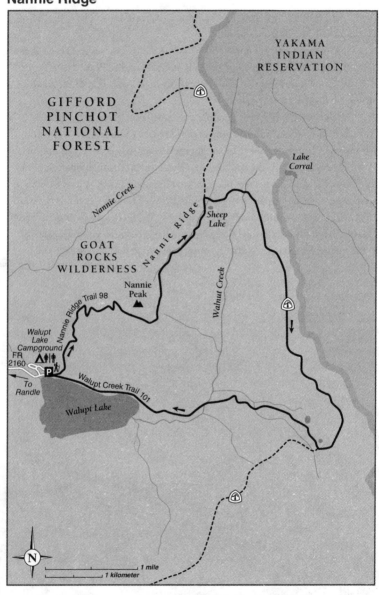

GIFFORD
PINCHOT
NATIONAL
FOREST

YAKAMA
INDIAN
RESERVATION

Nannie Creek

Lake
Corral

Nannie Ridge

Sheep
Lake

GOAT
ROCKS
WILDERNESS

Walnut Creek

Nannie
Peak

Nannie Ridge Trail 98

Walupt
Lake
Campground

FR
2160

P

To
Randle

Walupt Creek Trail 101

Walupt Lake

N

1 mile

1 kilometer

picture-perfect view of Mount Adams make it a popular camping destination for horsepackers, thru-hikers, and hikers on shorter trips.

Soon after you leave the lake on the Nannie Ridge Trail, you reach a junction with the Pacific Crest Trail (PCT). Follow the southbound trail around Sheep Lake toward the head of the Walupt Creek basin, where great views stretch to the south down the Walupt Creek valley.

The trail now descends through a mix of open and semiforested slopes. Around 8.5 miles, you spy the deep-blue water of Walupt Lake to the southwest. The trail continues to drop and then, at 10 miles, arrives at two small lakes that sit below Lakeview Mountain (6,660') and the junction with Walupt Creek Trail 101. Head west on the trail as it skirts the small lakes, passing several nice campsites.

After cresting a ridge, you begin a steep descent down tight switchbacks along a narrow ridgeline with creeks running on either side. The small amount of water that drains through this area creates a lush environment flourishing with ferns, vanilla leaf, and foamflower.

Two miles or so from the PCT turnoff, the trail crosses Walupt Creek. A couple of good campsites are located near the creek, but they may not have any water late in the season. Continue on through stands of Douglas-fir, and in another mile reach Walupt Lake's inlet creek. The last stretch follows the northern shoreline of the lake, which is a great place to stroll with kids if you're staying at the Walupt Lake Campground and looking for a brief outing. In another mile, the trail reaches the turnoff for Nannie Ridge and in a few hundred feet arrives back at the trailhead.

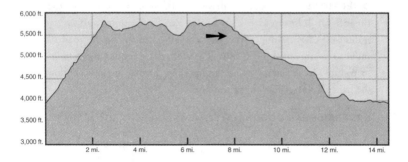

Mount Adams peeks through the trees near Sheep Lake.

PERMIT INFORMATION Northwest Forest Pass ($30/year) required; see tinyurl.com/northwestforestpass for more information. Self-issued permits available at the trailhead.

DIRECTIONS From Randle, drive east 13 miles on US 12 to the turnoff for Johnson Creek on Forest Road 21; the turnoff is 2.5 miles west of Packwood. Turn right (north) and follow the road 16 miles to the turnoff for FR 2160. Turn left, drive about 5 more miles to Walupt Creek Campground, and park in the day-use area. Follow the painted horseshoes to the trailhead.

GPS TRAILHEAD COORDINATES N46° 25.393' W121° 28.192'

6 Old Snowy Mountain

SCENERY: ✿ ✿ ✿ ✿ ✿	TRAIL CONDITION: ✿ ✿ ✿
CHILDREN: ✿	DIFFICULTY: ✿ ✿ ✿ ✿
SOLITUDE: ✿ ✿ ✿	DISTANCE: 26 miles
HIKING TIME: 2–3 days	GREEN TRAILS MAP: *White Pass 303*

OUTSTANDING FEATURES: Breathtaking views, "airy" sections of trail, alpine meadows, ancient glaciers, and a walk-up summit

WHEN I CHAT WITH NORTHWEST natives about Goat Rocks Wilderness, they often remark: "I've always wanted to go there." Well, go ahead and set foot in this awe-inspiring area, a favorite section for many Pacific Crest Trail (PCT) thru-hikers. The upper slopes of this hike can be snowbound well through July, so an ice axe and crampons may be necessary.

🚶🚶 Prepare for two things on this hike—jaw-dropping beauty and having to work for it. The trail begins at the rippling waters of North Fork Tieton and gains approximately 4,000 feet in 13 miles on its journey to the windswept summit of Old Snowy Mountain. If the distance or elevation seems daunting, there's an alternative approach from the much more popular southern route through Snowgrass Flats (cutting the distance in half). That said, the extra energy it takes to do the hike from this approach dramatically cuts the amount of traffic, and the trail leading to Old Snowy from the north will take your breath away.

The trail begins by immediately crossing North Fork Tieton River, more of a small creek than a raging river by late summer or fall. On the other side of the bridge, you enter Goat Rocks Wilderness, in which you'll remain for the duration of the hike. In less than 0.25 mile, you reach a junction. Take the right branch on Trail 1118 toward Tieton Pass. The other trail travels southeast on its long climb to Bear Creek Mountain.

From the junction, the trail gradually ascends, crossing a few small creeks along the way. At 1 mile, you reach a charming stream that pours down a

Old Snowy Mountain

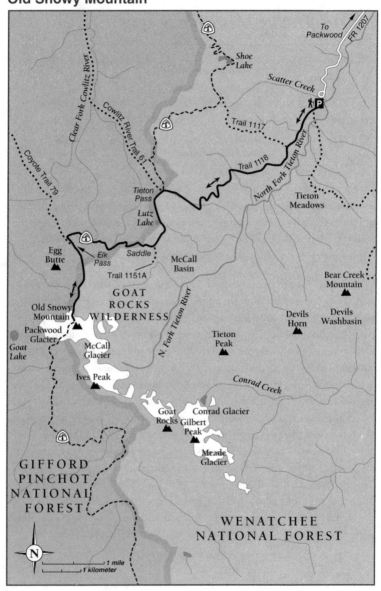

hanging garden then crosses the trail into a marshland full of vibrant, green horsetails. Just beyond here, you arrive at Trail 1117, a faint path easily overlooked if it weren't for the sign marking it. This trail takes off to the west and in 2.5 miles reaches the PCT 3 miles south of Tieton Pass. Remain on Trail 1118's more defined path, which gets you into Goat Rocks faster.

The trail continues its climb and is fairly ho-hum as it works its way through the woods before cresting a ridge 2.5 miles from the trailhead, your first real opportunity for open views. Devils Horns, Bear Creek Mountain, and Tieton Peak reveal themselves to the south, and as you drop back into the forest, knowing that the views are only going to improve, you might find a little pep in your step.

Another 1.5 miles brings you to the forested saddle of Tieton Pass, elevation 4,800 feet. The pass sits at a three-way junction, with the PCT running north and south and Cowlitz River Trail branching off to the northwest. Follow the PCT south as the trail meanders up, over, and around ribs, ridges, and small knolls. At 1.5 miles from Tieton Pass, you reach the shallow waters of Lutz Lake, a good place to camp, especially if you're traveling in a large group. It does make for a fairly long day hike to the summit of Old Snowy, but it also means not having to travel any farther with a heavy pack.

The trail skirts the lake and then begins a mellow climb to the turnoff for the wet meadows of McCall Basin, a popular spot to pitch a tent, especially for hunters who come here in the fall when the high hunt is open. If you're looking to escape some of the crowds (which aren't much of a problem

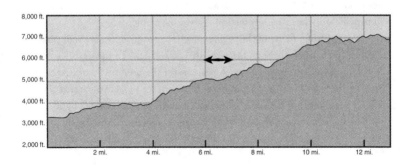

out here) and the weather is decent, continue another mile or two, to sites above treeline.

From the junction, the trail ascends a couple switchbacks then travels up a drainage with excellent views down into McCall Basin and southeast toward Tieton Peak. Just a couple more switchbacks and you're close to a saddle with a campsite tucked in a small stand of trees. The site provides a fairly nice shelter and could work in a pinch, but it as no water, and better sites are located farther up the trail. Just beyond the saddle, the trail crests the ridge and offers up views to the northwest, where you can catch a glimpse of Mount Rainier. The vista quickly disappears as the trail crosses back over to the south side of the ridge, working its way slightly below the summit of an unnamed knoll.

As the trail approaches a broad saddle, it's hard not to be moved by the beauty of this place, where hanging glaciers, cascading creeks, fields of wildflowers, and ancient peaks dominate the landscape. The trail descends from the saddle through a stand of alpine fir and hemlock, into a large basin. Just before the trail begins a steep climb, keep an eye out for a spur trail that takes off toward the creek, with a couple good campsites in a stand of trees near the water. This area is fragile, so please use existing sites and established trails to access them.

Continuing from the basin, the trail zigzags up a narrow rib and tops out at 6,000 feet on an expansive plateau. The path from here can be somewhat hard to follow because you have to cross creeks and snow patches along the way. A number of painted cairns every few hundred feet help ensure that you're going the right way. Tent sites—the last until the west flank of Old Snowy—are scattered across the plateau, but if the weather is poor, these sites will provide only minimal protection against the elements.

Moving along, the trail skirts a pyramid-shaped peak, where water has carved deep channels through the reddish-brown rock. To the west lies the Elk Pass snowfield, where you can sometimes see the boot tracks of hikers who glissaded through the snow. From here, the main trail takes you across glacially striated bedrock before it ascends to a saddle just below Peak 6768.

The trail traverses below the peak's rugged ridgeline, crossing the exposed north face, where snow can linger well into summer. The scene from here is spectacular, with the Clear Fork of the Cowlitz River canyon to the north and the gleaming slopes of Mount Rainier in the distance. The trail continues to wrap around to the southwest and soon enters a stand of weatherbeaten white bark pines. As you exit the stand of trees, you arrive at Elk Pass (6,700') and enter the heart of Goat Rocks Wilderness.

From the pass, Coyote Trail 79 branches off toward Upper Lake Creek canyon, which funnels water from all of the steep creeks and long, narrow waterfalls that pour from the snowfields above. Continue south on the PCT along an exciting section of trail constructed in 1953 and 1954. As you resume your hike from the pass, the trail works its way up a broad, mellow ridge with stunning views south toward the McCall Glacier and Old Snowy's pointed summit.

This next section is somewhat "airy" and can be intimidating; the trail is never as bad as it looks from a distance, however. It should be noted that many of these slopes can be snowbound well into July, and an ice axe and crampons may be required. That said, this is also the most stunning section of the hike because it travels along a jagged, narrow ridgeline.

The headwaters of Upper Lake Creek Canyon

The first exposed slope runs along a narrow footpath below Peak 7210's talus to a small, narrow saddle, where you can see Tieton Peak and Devils Horns due east of Old Snowy. From the saddle, the trail seems to disappear, but a somewhat indiscernible path takes off to the right and quickly reveals itself through loose, broken rock as the main trail. Continue along the ridge until you reach a crest saddle on the south side of Old Snowy.

From here, you have a couple of options. The PCT used to travel up and over the summit of Old Snowy (7,930'), and the remnants of the old trail are still visible from this location. The climber's trail ascends 0.6 mile and gains approximately 550 feet. If you still have the itch to explore, drop off the northern shoulder and switchback west to rejoin the PCT.

If the weather is bad or you have had enough excitement for one day, continue on the official PCT route that was blasted by the U.S. Forest Service in 1978. The route runs above the Packwood Glacier to the second-highest point on the PCT in Washington. Once again, the view is impressive. The emerald waters of Goat Lake, to the northwest, contrast strikingly with the deep reds, greens, and grays of the slopes surrounding it. Snap some photos and revel in the great scenery before retracing your steps back to camp.

PERMIT INFORMATION Northwest Forest Pass ($30/year) required; see tinyurl.com/northwestforestpass for more information. Self-issued permits available at the trailhead.

DIRECTIONS From Packwood, drive east 19 miles on WA 12 to White Pass. Continue 7.5 miles and turn right on Forest Road 1200—a sign on the highway for Clear Lake marks the turn. Follow the paved road approximately 3 miles, and just as it begins to make a sharp curve, continue straight on Forest Road 1207. Follow this dirt road another 5 miles or so to its end at the trailhead, where there is ample parking.

GPS TRAILHEAD COORDINATES
N46° 34.512' W121° 21.487'

7 Round Mountain

SCENERY: ✿ ✿ ✿	TRAIL CONDITION: ✿ ✿ ✿
CHILDREN: ✿ ✿	DIFFICULTY: ✿ ✿ ✿
SOLITUDE: ✿ ✿ ✿ ✿	DISTANCE: 12 miles
HIKING TIME: 6–7 hours	GREEN TRAILS MAP: *White Pass 303*

OUTSTANDING FEATURES: Great views into Goat Rocks Wilderness, a somewhat "warm" alpine lake to swim around in, and the chance to stand on top of two different peaks

A SIGN ON POPULAR WHITE PASS reads RECREATION NEXT 23 MILES, a dead giveaway to the main attraction. It should, therefore, come as no surprise that the parking lot for the Pacific Crest Trail (PCT) can be packed on any given weekend. Anglers, hunters, and hikers come from all around to explore the vast wilderness that surrounds this path. When I ventured on to the quiet, albeit steep, Twin Peaks Trail, I was more than pleasantly surprised not to see another soul on a warm, sunny Friday afternoon.

🚶🚶 One of my favorite things is stumbling upon new areas right in my own backyard. I roped in a longtime local to do this hike with me, and as we laced our boots and stuffed our packs, I discovered that she had never hiked this trail. Easily bypassed by those wishing to remain on the PCT, this little side trail is a great place to avoid the crowds and take in some spectacular vistas.

From the parking area, head southbound on the PCT. The trail immediately crosses the south fork of Clear Creek, where a jaunt upstream eventually leads to Leech Lake. Conveniently located just north of US 12, the lake is a popular horse-camping destination and an access point for those traveling north on the PCT.

Continuing past the creek, the trail steadily climbs long, gradual switchbacks through stands of second-growth forests. At 1.3 miles, the trail passes a small stream whose waters flow into, instead of out of, Leech Lake. You walk only briefly along the stream bank before turning back into the cool shade of

Round Mountain

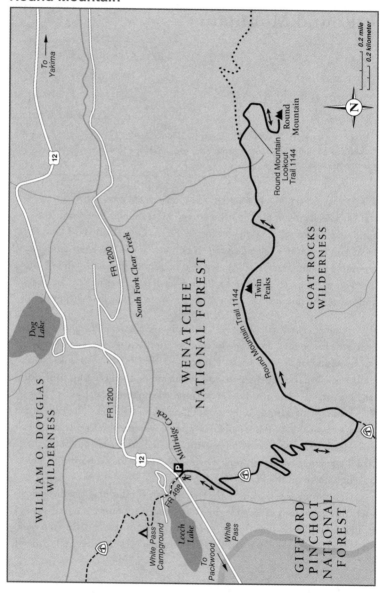

WILLIAM O. DOUGLAS WILDERNESS

Dog Lake

To Yakima

12

FR 1200

South Fork Clear Creek

FR 1200

WENATCHEE NATIONAL FOREST

GOAT ROCKS WILDERNESS

Round Mountain

Round Mountain Lookout Trail 1144

Twin Peaks

Round Mountain Trail 1144

Millridge Creek

12

P

FR 1698

White Pass Campground

Leech Lake

White Pass

To Packwood

GIFFORD PINCHOT NATIONAL FOREST

0.2 mile
0.2 kilometer

N

the forest. In another 0.5 mile, two large boulder fields provide ample seating for anyone wishing to take a load off and enjoy a little sun.

From here, the trail reenters the forest and soon enters Goat Rocks Wilderness. Just beyond the sign, you pass Ginnette Lake, a swimming hole with decent camping. The trail turns east and passes a boggy pond. Keep an eye out for Round Mountain Trail 1144. The sign for the trail sits high up in a tree, on the left-hand side, and is somewhat easy to miss if you're not paying attention.

When you get to the junction, turn northeast off the well-traveled PCT, and join the trail to Round Mountain, which begins with a short, steep descent to a lush meadow before flattening out as it wraps around a small point. Enjoy the level ground while it lasts because your first of a few climbs is about to begin.

The path to the first of the Twin Peaks begins on a mellow gradient that slowly works its way to a saddle. From here, the trail shoots straight up the ridge, sending your heart rate straight up as well. I used the excuse of hiking with a local to stop every few minutes and catch my breath as she told me about the views that were beginning to open on our ascent up the ridge. To the southwest lies Hogback Ridge, where you can see the PCT in the hillside just below the ridge as it continues south toward the heart of Goat Rocks Wilderness.

Resuming your climb, enjoy the multiplying views: the manicured runs of White Pass Ski Area to the west; the rugged, glaciated slopes of Old Snowy Mountain, Ives Peak, and Mount Curtis Gilbert to the southwest; and the craggy ridgelines of Bear Creek Mountain and Devils Horns to the south.

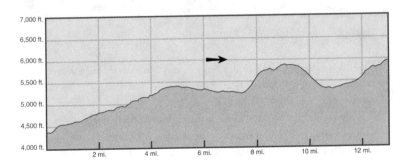

A windswept saddle lies below the summit of Twin Peaks.

The trail runs just below the peak's summit and descends through a steep, loose scree field to a prominent, windswept saddle. Dog Lake is to the north, at the base of Spiral Butte's conical slopes.

From the saddle, the trail ascends through a stand of scraggly trees, crosses a small saddle, and switches to the north side of the ridge. It then travels below the second of the two peaks as it begins a 500-foot descent to a broad, forested saddle. The trail stays relatively level for 0.5 mile or so—a nice break from the ups and downs you've endured to this point. The uniformity of the woods is quickly interrupted by an entire hillside covered in small rocks and boulders. The trail makes a couple of small switchbacks along the flanks of the rocky slope before reentering the woods.

At 5.5 miles from the trailhead, you reach the turnoff for Round Mountain Lookout Trail 1144A. If you want to thru-hike, continue east another 2 miles to Forest Road 840. It's approximately 14.7 miles from the PCT trailhead to the Round Mountain Trailhead via WA 12 and Tieton Road/FR 1207. Continuing from the junction, head north up another series of switchbacks until you reach the abandoned fire lookout of Round Mountain, elevation 5,970 feet.

U.S. Forest Service employees stationed at the lookout (erected in the 1930s) monitored the area's frequent fires. The lookout was disassembled in 1976 when other methods of fire monitoring were established. Even without the lookout, the views from this perch make the climb well worth the effort. Mount Adams reveals itself for the first time to the south, and Clear and Rimrock Lakes, to the east, twinkle in the afternoon light. Views to the north are somewhat obscured; however, a little maneuvering allows a glimpse of Mount Rainier. Tired and a little on the dusty side, you'll want to take a dip in the refreshing waters of Ginnette Lake on the hike back out.

PERMIT INFORMATION Northwest Forest Pass ($30/year) required; see tinyurl.com/northwestforestpass for more information.

DIRECTIONS From Packwood, follow WA 12 east 19 miles to White Pass. The trailhead is on the south side of the road, approximately 0.5 mile from White Pass Village.

GPS TRAILHEAD COORDINATES N46° 38.052' W121° 19.846'

Central: White Pass to Stevens Pass

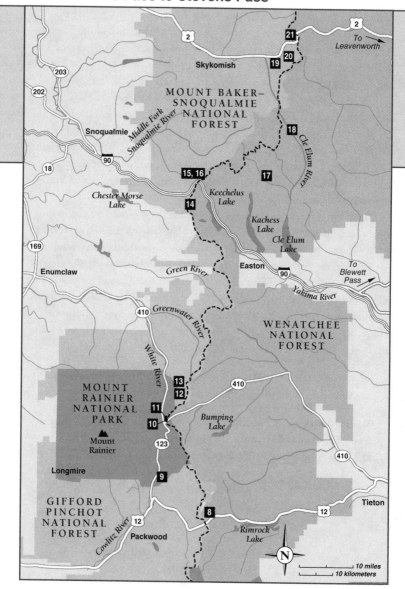

PART 2: CENTRAL

White Pass to Stevens Pass

Mount Rainier from Sourdough Gap (see Hike 11, page 83)

8 Buesch and Dumbbell Lakes

SCENERY: ✿ ✿ ✿

CHILDREN: ✿ ✿ ✿ ✿

SOLITUDE: ✿ ✿ ✿

HIKING TIME: 1–2 days

TRAIL CONDITION: ✿ ✿ ✿ ✿

DIFFICULTY: ✿ ✿ ✿

DISTANCE: 16 miles

GREEN TRAILS MAP: White Pass 303

OUTSTANDING FEATURES: A plethora of lakes to visit, an awesome location to take kids camping for their first time, and moderate elevation gain and loss

ONE WORD OF CAUTION ABOUT this hike: *bugs*! While alpine lakes are the perfect place for us humans to hang out, the swampy marshlands and stagnant ponds that surround them provide the ideal environment for mosquitoes and other biting insects. If you can find the time in late summer or fall, save this hike for the off-season. Otherwise, make sure you bring plenty of mosquito netting, and consider doing the loop over the course of a moderately long day.

One of the many small lakes that dot the William O. Douglas Wilderness

👣 You have two options for starting this hike. The first option is to take off from the Pacific Crest Trail (PCT) trailhead, which is 0.5 mile northeast of White Pass on the north side of US 12. This trailhead is very popular with equestrians and can be packed on the weekend. A somewhat quieter option is to start from Dog Lake Campground, another 1.5 miles east past the turnoff for the PCT, on the north side of the road. There's enough room for only four vehicles, so if the parking spaces are taken, you might find yourself backtracking to the PCT trailhead.

Regardless of which trailhead you begin from, take a detailed map—you have a ton of options once you hit the northern lakes, and deciding which way to go can be a bit confusing. Whichever way you go, the terrain is anything but disappointing.

Leaving from Dog Lake Campground, follow the trailhead sign for Cramer Lake, and you soon reach the junction for Dark Meadows Trail 1107. Turn east and follow the trail up a steep incline that will leave you second-guessing my conclusion that this is a mellow hike. Not to worry: the gradient eases off in less than 1 mile, and the trail resumes an enjoyable pitch as you stroll through the William O. Douglas Wilderness. This section seemed neglected—there were a few downed trees that were easy enough to negotiate on foot but could cause problems for someone traveling with a horse or llama.

The trail crosses a small stream and begins a slight ascent as it makes its way to the junction with the PCT. From here, it's 1.3 miles south to US 12, but take the northbound trail, which contours to the east on its way to Deer Lake. Prepare for a steady yet gradual ascent as you leave the junction on your way toward the first of many lakes. In 0.5 mile, the trail passes a small, grassy meadow, where it levels out for a bit. Take some time to catch your breath, and enjoy the sound of the water flowing through this area. Beyond the meadow, you'll follow and then cross an outlet stream for Deer Lake before arriving at a larger meadow full of low-lying huckleberry bushes, tall grasses, and alpine fir and hemlock.

Just as the trail begins to reenter the forest, you'll notice a path that branches off to the south. This side trail will lead you to a camp at the southern end of Deer Lake. Proximity to US 12 makes this pretty little lake a very

Buesch and Dumbbell Lakes

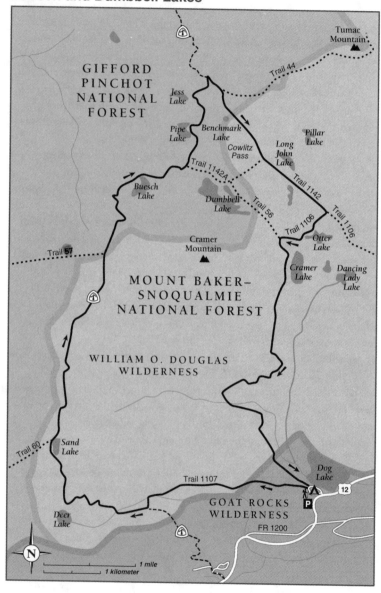

GIFFORD
PINCHOT
NATIONAL
FOREST

*Tumac
Mountain*

Trail 44

*Jess
Lake*

*Pipe
Lake*

*Benchmark
Lake*

*Cowlitz
Pass*

*Pillar
Lake*

*Long
John
Lake*

Trail 1142A

Trail 1142

Trail 1106

*Buesch
Lake*

*Dumbbell
Lake*

Trail 56

Trail 57

*Cramer
Mountain*

*Otter
Lake*

*Cramer
Lake*

*Dancing
Lady
Lake*

MOUNT BAKER–
SNOQUALMIE
NATIONAL FOREST

WILLIAM O. DOUGLAS
WILDERNESS

Trail 60

*Sand
Lake*

Trail 1107

*Dog
Lake*

12

*Deer
Lake*

GOAT ROCKS
WILDERNESS

FR 1200

P

N

1 mile

1 kilometer

popular place to camp. Hitching posts and extremely large sites also reveal the amount of horse traffic this area sees. The lake is well liked for a reason, so if you happen to be here when no one is around, you may want to consider staying put for the night.

Continuing on the PCT, the trail contours north from the lake turnoff and follows a slight rise above the large meadow, where a small pond can be seen tucked among the tall, swaying grass. Soon you arrive at aptly named Sand Lake. The impact of campers at this well-liked campsite is less noticeable, and so are the people. A spur trail at the base of the lake's peninsula leads to a small shelter.

Just beyond the spur on the west side of the lake is a junction with Sand Lake Trail 60, which heads south 2.8 miles to Forest Road 1284. The PCT continues north through an old burn, where grayish-black snags contrast strikingly with purple lupines and bright-green grasslands. In another mile or so, the trail passes a large boulder with a series of dinner plate–like rocks stacked neatly on top of it. As you round the corner, you get a good glimpse east toward Spiral Butte and Clear Lake.

The next few miles are fairly uninteresting; however, the easy walking makes the time go by fast. Just more than 6 miles along, the trail meets up with Cortright Creek Trail 57, a quiet, obscure route that takes you 4.5 miles west to FR 45. Remain heading north on the well-traveled PCT, where ponds, puddles, mud holes, and lakes continue to dominate the landscape. A small pass provides a change of scenery, as views open to the northwest, where Fryingpan Mountain rises above the forested ridgelines in the distance.

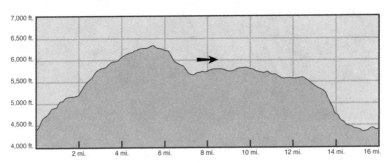

Layered rocks in the William O. Douglas Wilderness

The trail remains relatively flat for the next mile or so. Two descending switchbacks lead you to the Buesch Lake basin, where you're first greeted with a scattering of small ponds in an expansive field of tall grass that shimmers in the wind. As you cross the outlet stream at 7.5 miles, you get a good view of the lake. The grassy shoreline makes it difficult to access the water, and better camping can be found farther down the line.

Head east from the lake and soon arrive at a junction. You have a couple of options from this point, but all of them eventually lead you back to where you started. Traveling east, in less than 0.5 mile you reach Dumbbell Lake, one of the larger bodies of water in this area. From there, head south toward Cramer Lake, and in about 5 miles, you reach your starting point.

If you're feeling motivated, you can add a 2.5-mile miniloop to your hike by continuing north on the PCT to Pipe Lake, whose northern shore boasts great camping. A short way north of the lake is Cowlitz Trail 44. Take this trail east, and in 0.2 mile, you arrive at another decision-making point. Those of you who, like me, crave open, 360-degree views, should take the not-so-well-maintained but well-worth-the-effort Tumac Mountain Trail. Be prepared to sweat, though, because this little out-and-back adds another 3.4 miles and 1,100 feet of elevation gain.

Venturing on from the junction, Shellrock Lake Trail 1142 heads south-east and quickly comes to Benchmark Lake. This murky-looking pond has, for some reason, earned a name for itself—quite possibly because it lies just beyond a U.S. Geological Survey marker that sits on a rock just off the trail. In another 0.5 mile, you reach the clear waters of Long John Lake, whose grassy shores provide the perfect habitat for a wide range of birds. This spot is a bird lover's paradise, and quiet campsites dot the area.

Just beyond the lake is Long John Trail 1142A, which heads east to reach Dumbbell Lake in 0.7 mile. You can also continue southeast past, you guessed it, more puddles and ponds, to a junction that lies just beyond a section of trail that cuts through grassland. Turn off onto Cramer Lake Trail 1106 and head to the junction that takes you to Dumbbell Lake, as described above. Upon reaching the junction, turn south; the trail soon passes Cramer Lake. The route is a few hundred yards up from the lake, but you'll find paths leading to good camping closer to the shoreline.

The next portion of trail remains in the forest, for the most part. A couple of open sections provide views of Spiral Butte's rocky west-facing slopes and Dog Lake's deep-blue waters to the south. As you continue your descent, you can hear the grumble of the north fork of a creek that feeds into Dog Lake. This is your last major obstacle of the hike—there's no bridge at the crossing, so you'll have to wade through the cold water. Use caution: the rocks are extremely slippery even if the water is low. If you're at all concerned with water levels, it might be a good idea to do this hike in the opposite direction in case high water requires you to turn around.

Less than 2 miles from the crossing is the junction with Dark Meadows Trail, which you started out on. It's just a few hundred yards to the trailhead and, yes, there's another lake for you to enjoy!

PERMIT INFORMATION Northwest Forest Pass ($30/year) required; see tinyurl.com/northwestforestpass for more information. Self-issued permits available at the trailhead.

DIRECTIONS From Packwood, follow WA 12 east 19 miles to White Pass. Continue 2 miles farther and turn left into Dog Lake Campground. Follow the one-way loop to the trailhead parking area.

GPS TRAILHEAD COORDINATES N46° 39.145' W121° 21.659'

9 Laughingwater Creek

SCENERY: ✿ ✿ ✿   TRAIL CONDITION: ✿ ✿ ✿ ✿

CHILDREN: ✿ ✿   DIFFICULTY: ✿ ✿ ✿

SOLITUDE: ✿ ✿ ✿ ✿   DISTANCE: 12–20 miles

HIKING TIME: 1–2 days

GREEN TRAILS MAPS: *Mount Rainier East 270 and Bumping Lake 271*

OUTSTANDING FEATURES: Three Lakes, Two Lakes, green lakes, blue lakes—what more could you want? How about stunning views of Mount Rainier, ample huckleberry picking, and excellent wildlife-viewing opportunities?

WHEN THEY THINK OF MOUNT RAINIER National Park, most people simply envision the mountain, with its broken glaciers and rugged volcanic outcroppings. While the dramatic images are impressive, the park has a softer side that usually goes unnoticed. This is your chance to experience a place where mist rises from calm, clear lakes that lie in thick, old-growth forests; brightly colored dragonflies dance on the water's edge; and bull elk can be heard bugling during the rutting season on a crisp fall afternoon.

🚶🚶 One of the great things about this hike is that you have a few ways to do it. Depending on how much time, energy, and motivation you have, you can either hike the 6 miles into Three Lakes, have lunch, and head back out; pitch a tent at Three Lakes and do Two Lakes as a day hike; or take your time and spend a night at each lake. Note that Three Lakes is within the national park boundary, where firearms, pets, and campfires are prohibited. Also, if you decide to camp there, make sure to stop by any of the park's visitor information centers to obtain a backcountry permit.

To begin, head east, crossing WA 123, to a small post that marks the trailhead for Laughingwater Creek. The trail starts off in an old-growth forest, where minute pinecones and thousands of needles cover the forest floor, creating a soft, cushy surface. In a little less than 1 mile, the trail gains a ridge and you can hear Laughingwater Creek giggling in a deep gorge far below.

Laughingwater Creek

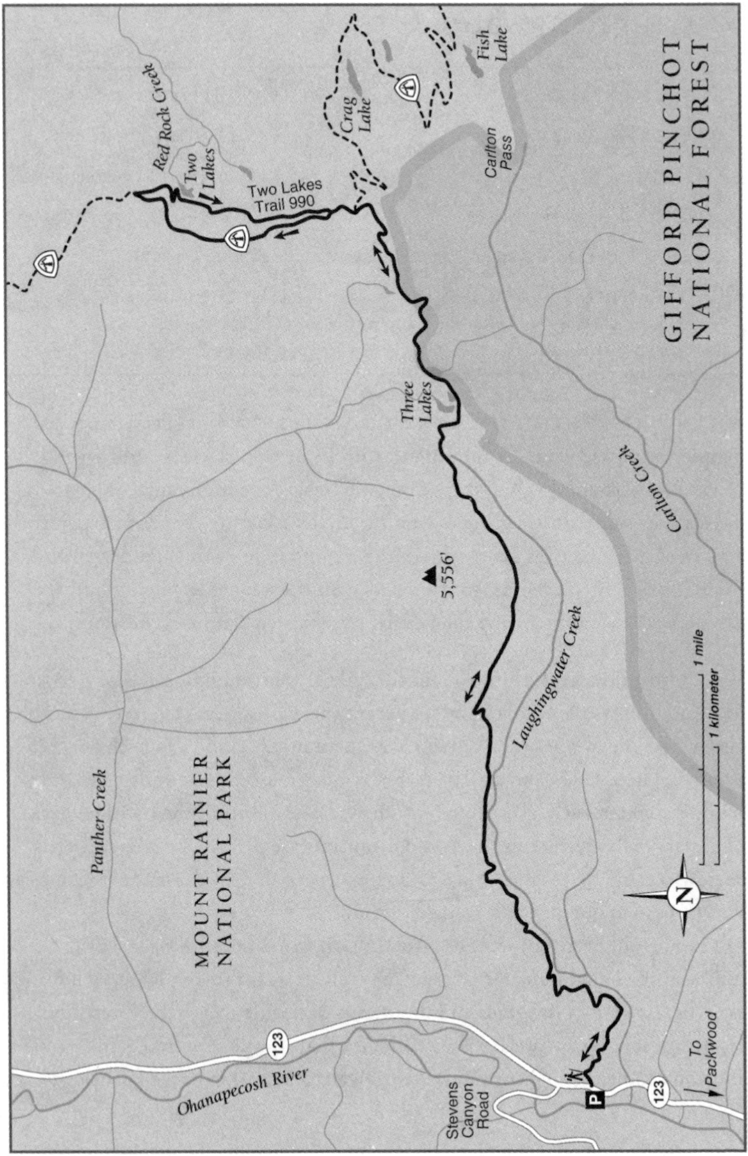

GIFFORD PINCHOT NATIONAL FOREST

Fish Lake

Crag Lake

Carlton Pass

Red Rock Creek

Two Lakes

Two Lakes Trail 990

Carlton Creek

Three Lakes

5,556'

Laughingwater Creek

Panther Creek

MOUNT RAINIER NATIONAL PARK

1 mile

1 kilometer

N

Ohanapecosh River

123

Stevens Canyon Road

P

To Packwood

123

Follow the ridge proper a short distance before the trail drops then crests a forested plateau.

After enjoying level ground for a bit, you follow the trail down a few gentle switchbacks to a spot where you can see the creek for the first time. The path leaves the creek and soon passes a grassy pond, which you briefly glimpse through the thick vegetation before you resume your ever-steady climb toward Three Lakes.

In 1 mile or so, the trail levels out, and you find yourself walking beside the gentle waters of Laughingwater Creek. This pleasant section is filled with enormous Douglas-firs and trickling feeder streams with wooden footbridges. As you wander along, take note of the huge rounds cut out of the trail by a hardworking trail crew. They make good seats, so consider taking a short break before beginning another fairly long uphill push.

From here, the trail climbs away from the creek as it follows around the southeast side of point 5556. Along the way, it crosses steep ravines and rocky creeks that plunge into the drainage below. The trail continues traveling through old-growth forests and occasionally crosses open slopes that allow for brief glimpses of the surrounding hillsides.

At approximately 5.5 miles, the trail tops out and enters the first of a series of lush meadows and reaches the former junction with the unmaintained, extremely hard to find East Boundary Trail. (Current Green Trails maps no longer show it.) Continue on the main trail and begin a 0.5-mile descent to Three Lakes.

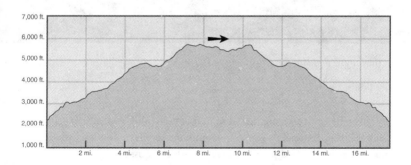

A stunning view of Mount Rainier from the PCT

The first two lakes are tucked in next to each other and, at first glance, look as if they are one. As you wrap around the southernmost lake, you'll notice a newly restored park service cabin, which houses backcountry rangers, trail crews, and other park service employees who work in the area. This camp is one of only four within the park that allow horses. Two designated camp-sites and one group site are uphill from the cabin.

The third and largest of the lakes is reached in another 0.2 mile. As you approach it, you leave the park and enter the William O. Douglas Wilderness. Backcountry permits are not required here, so if the sites are full at the first two lakes, this is a feasible option. Whether or not you camp here, this lake has the best opportunities for swimming and should be explored.

Leaving the lake, the trail travels below a rocky knoll, giving it an alpine feel as it ascends toward the Pacific Crest Trail (PCT). Soon you reenter the national park boundary. From the boundary line, the trail crosses a flat, grassy section before reentering the forest. A small pond tucked beside a stand of trees breaks up the monotony of the forest, as do the lupines that litter the forest floor.

In another mile, the trail reaches a saddle with a small unnamed lake and your first opportunity for open views of Mount Rainier. Camping is prohibited at the lake; however, it's a great day-hike option from the Three Lakes camp if you don't feel like hiking all the way to Two Lakes. The trail ascends from the lake and, in 0.25 mile, reaches a creek that's dry and dusty by late summer. After a couple of switchbacks, the trail follows alongside the drainage then crosses the creek at its headwaters, which is nothing more than a concave meadow by the time summer rolls around.

In less than 0.25 mile, you reach the junction with the PCT—and what a spectacular junction it is! Mount Rainier's crevasse-ridden glaciers dominate the foreground, almost making you overlook Mounts Adams and St. Helens towering proudly in the distance. The vistas are impressive from here on as you work your way onto a ridge, where you'll get a bird's-eye view of Bumping Lake to the northeast.

Just 0.3 mile from the junction with the PCT, you reach a large viewing area and an unmarked junction with Two Lakes Trail 990, which eventually leads you to Two Lakes. You can then make a small loop back to the PCT. Since the trail is tricky to find from this direction, continue on the PCT to the well-marked northern entrance and come back out on this trail.

Views like this make the long climb into the alpine well worth the effort.

Heading north on the PCT, the trail slips over to the east side of the divide, running below a ridgeline of short, stubby pillars of rock. After you crest the ridge, a decent-sized watering hole, aptly named One Lake, comes into view. This is a great spot to view wildlife, so if you have the time and the patience, it may be worth hanging out here with a pair of binoculars on a lazy afternoon. Continuing on, the trail soon enters a small stand of trees and exits east through a bowl.

As the trail turns north again, keep an eye out for the Two Lakes junction. Once there, turn south, and begin to descend the steep, rutted trail. Don't get discouraged: the trail quickly improves, and in 0.3 mile, you reach the lake. Excellent camping is available here, and permits are *not* required. To make the loop back to the PCT, continue around the western shore of the lake and follow the trail south. The path is easy to follow, and in less than a mile, you'll be back at the large viewing area just off the PCT.

PERMIT INFORMATION Because the trailhead is outside of a park entrance station, you don't have to pay a fee. A backcountry permit is required, however, at Three Lakes; use designated campsites. Make reservations (see nps.gov/mora/planyourvisit/wilderness-permit.htm for details) or register in person at the Ohanapecosh Visitor Center (360-569-6581) during operating hours.

DIRECTIONS Follow WA 12 east from Packwood 7.6 miles, and turn left onto WA 123. Continue north 5.2 miles, passing Ohanapecosh Campground and Ohanapecosh Visitor Center and crossing the Laughingwater Creek Bridge; look for a pulloff on the left side of the road, about 0.1 mile from the bridge. If you miss the pulloff, the closest place to turn around is the Stevens Canyon park entrance station, 0.1 mile ahead on the left.

GPS TRAILHEAD COORDINATES N46° 45.101' W121° 33.432'

10 Dewey Lake

SCENERY: ✿ ✿ ✿ ✿	TRAIL CONDITION: ✿ ✿ ✿
CHILDREN: ✿ ✿ ✿ ✿	DIFFICULTY: ✿ ✿ ✿
SOLITUDE: ✿ ✿	HIKING TIME: 3–5 hours

DISTANCE: 8 miles (includes walking around lake)

GREEN TRAILS MAPS: *Mount Rainier East 270 and Bumping Lake 271*

OUTSTANDING FEATURES: Alpine vistas in all directions, great views of
Mount Rainier, and abundant camping along the peaceful shores of Dewey Lake

THE TRAILS LEAVING FROM CHINOOK PASS are usually packed
with people on the weekends. An awe-inspiring drive, easy access to spectacular alpine scenery, and an entrance point to Mount Rainier National Park
are the main draws, rain or shine. Don't be discouraged by the crowds; there's
enough amazing terrain for everyone to enjoy.

𝕏 From the parking lot, head south to the trailhead, which is marked
by a large interpretive sign that discusses the various trails in the area. Pick up
the Pacific Crest Trail (PCT) just beyond this point, and continue south
0.3 mile until you reach a junction. This hike can be done in either direction; however, I recommend starting out on the PCT for the grand views
of Mount Rainier toward the end of the hike and good vistas of Dewey Lake
before you descend to its shores.

If you decide to travel this way, continue east on the PCT across
a wooden overpass that crosses WA 410, marking the top of Chinook Pass at
5,400 feet and the boundary between Mount Rainier National Park and
the Wenatchee National Forest. In 0.25 mile, the trail enters the William
O. Douglas Wilderness, named after a US Supreme Court justice and
Washington native who spent many of his summers exploring this vast area
from the small mountain town of Goose Prairie.

Upon entering the wilderness, the trail travels southwest and skirts the
northeast side of Naches Peak. A little less than 1 mile into the hike, the trail
reaches a small tarn that sits among alpine benches. If you decide to take a

break here, or just want to find a good place for your tripod, use existing trails when exploring the area.

From here, the trail continues its ascent through stunning alpine meadows, with fantastic views to the southeast of an unnamed pyramid-shaped peak. What was once a mighty mountain has been eroded into a pyramid of loose rock and scree fields that range in color from deep orange to smoky gray. Views continue to open as you approach a small pass that leads to an overlook of Dewey Lake, situated below the daunting, steep slopes of Seymour Peak. Many people are content with this vantage point and follow the Naches Peak Loop Trail back to Chinook Pass.

If you want to extend your hike or are perhaps looking for a short overnight trip, continue south along the PCT just more than 1 mile to Dewey Lake. If you decide to camp, be aware that no fires are allowed within 0.25 mile of the lake. As you begin your descent, watch your ankles: the trail works its way across open slopes, and there's lots of loose rock scattered in the path. Soon the trail switchbacks to enter a thick, dark stand of trees. The view may not be the most exciting, but the trail evens out and turns into a pleasant stroll. At 2.7 miles, the trail crosses several boardwalks that keep the path elevated above areas of fragile vegetation.

As you approach the lake, you pass a creek that leads to the small lake west of Dewey Lake. The lake itself is not too impressive; however, the wildflowers that surround it are worth checking out. Once you have taken your fair share of photos, continue along the PCT to reach the shores of Dewey Lake. The descent to the lake is well worth the extra effort, and those who simply enjoy its beauty from the viewpoint above miss out on the fields of wildflowers that surround the lake during peak season.

If you want more, check out the trail that circles the lake, adding 2 miles to the hike. Continue along the PCT 0.7 mile until you reach a junction where the PCT heads south to Anderson Lake. Take Dewey Way Trail 968A, and in 0.3 mile, reach a bridge. Cross the bridge, and in a few hundred feet you'll see an unmaintained spur trail that heads around the north side of the lake 0.8 mile. Trail 968 descends into the American River drainage, which eventually rejoins WA 410.

Dewey Lake

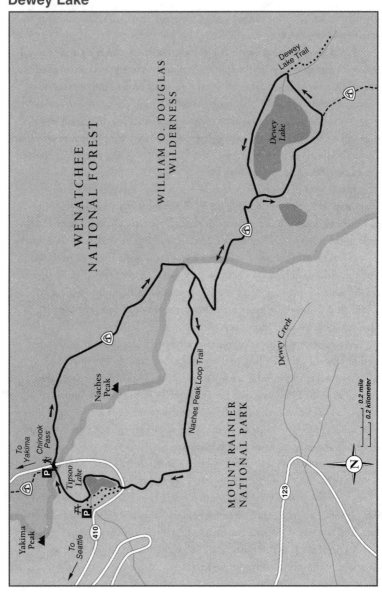

Dewey Lake Trail

Dewey Lake

WENATCHEE NATIONAL FOREST

WILLIAM O. DOUGLAS WILDERNESS

Naches Peak

Naches Peak Loop Trail

MOUNT RAINIER NATIONAL PARK

Dewey Creek

To Yakima

Chinook Pass

Yakima Peak

Tipsoo Lake

To Seattle

410

123

N

0.2 mile
0.2 kilometer

Once you have made the complete loop around the lake, continue back up the PCT to the junction with Naches Peak Loop Trail, and follow it west toward Tipsoo Lake. Soon you'll enter Mount Rainier National Park and get your first glimpse of Mount Rainier itself. The views are impressive as the trail drops off a ridge and passes a small lake that sits among another great field of wildflowers. On a calm day, Rainier's Emmons Glacier is reflected in the still waters.

From here, the terrain begins to change, with alpine meadows being replaced with stands of subalpine fir and mountain ash as you make your way down to WA 410 and Tipsoo Lake. Use caution as you cross the busy road to reach the trailhead on the other side. Follow the trail around the shore of upper Tipsoo Lake in either direction until you arrive at a picnic area. Take an immediate right out of the picnic area and ascend quickly above the lakes into a thick stand of trees that top out in a small, open meadow. Just on the other side of the meadow, you'll reach the WA 410 overpass and the end of the loop. Head north on the PCT back to the parking lot.

PERMIT INFORMATION Northwest Forest Pass ($30/year) required; see tinyurl.com/northwestforestpass for more information. Self-issued permits available at the trailhead.

DIRECTIONS

FROM SEATTLE: From I-405 just east of I-5, drive 2 miles east to WA 167; then drive 20 miles south to WA 410. Follow WA 410 east for 37 miles to the small town of Greenwater; from here, it's 5 more

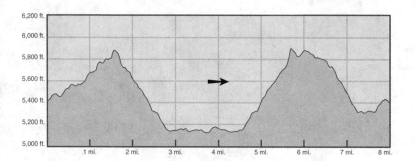

miles to the entrance of Mount Rainier National Park. Drive 18 miles past the park entrance and, just before WA 410 meets WA 123, bear left (east) to stay on WA 410. Drive 3.7 miles to Chinook Pass, and park in the large lot on the left (west) side of the road.

FROM TACOMA: From WA 512 just east of I-5, drive 14 miles east to WA 167. Bear right and, in 1 mile, turn right on WA 167. Drive 20 miles south to WA 410, and follow the remaining directions above.

FROM YAKIMA: From US 12 just west of I-82, drive 17 miles west. Where US 12 heads south at the T in Naches, continue west for 46 miles on WA 410 to Chinook Pass. Park in the large lot on the right (west) side of the road.

GPS TRAILHEAD COORDINATES N46° 52.483' W121° 31.081'

Alpine country surrounds Dewey Lake.

11 Sheep Lake and Sourdough Gap

> SCENERY: ✿ ✿ ✿ ✿
>
> TRAIL CONDITION: ✿ ✿ ✿ ✿ ✿
>
> CHILDREN: ✿ ✿ ✿ ✿ ✿
>
> DIFFICULTY: ✿ ✿
>
> SOLITUDE: ✿ ✿
>
> HIKING TIME: 3–5 hours
>
> DISTANCE: 6.4 miles round-trip to Sourdough Gap
>
> GREEN TRAILS MAPS: *Mount Rainier East 270 and Bumping Lake 271*
>
> OUTSTANDING FEATURES: Alpine lake, fields of colorful wildflowers in late July and August, short, easy hike for kids, and dramatic glimpses of Mount Rainier near Sourdough Gap

THIS POPULAR TRAIL FROM CHINOOK PASS heads north from the same trailhead parking lot as the Dewey Lake hike. This is a great introductory backpack for children or anyone else who is looking to "get their feet wet." If you plan to camp here, be aware that Sheep Lake sits at 5,800 feet, so nights can be chilly, no matter what time of year it is.

🏃 From the parking lot, head north along the PCT. From the moment your feet hit the trail, you're immersed in fields of wildflowers—beargrass, scarlet paintbrush, and columbine, to name just a few. The trail parallels the highway for the first mile; however, the colorful hillside distracts you from the traffic below. At 1.3 miles, the trail turns north and enters the cool shade of the forest, while the highway begins its eastern descent toward Pleasant Valley. From here, the trail meanders through alpine fir trees and meadows of lupine as it gains the last 300 feet to Sheep Lake.

The trail tops out along the lake's southern shores. A flat, sandy spot among large boulders is a great place to have lunch or take a nap in the afternoon sun. This spot is extremely popular on weekends or sunny, warm weekdays, so plan to share your break with others. The lake is the perfect place to take kids on a short overnight backpacking trip, and there's a good chance that they will have other kids to run around and explore with. If you decide to take some time and enjoy the alpine beauty, please help protect this fragile area by using some basic Leave No Trace principles: take breaks in areas that

Sheep Lake and Sourdough Gap

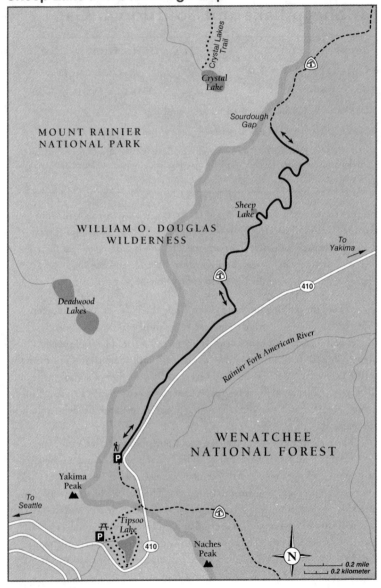

Crystal Lakes Trail

Crystal Lake

MOUNT RAINIER NATIONAL PARK

Sourdough Gap

Sheep Lake

WILLIAM O. DOUGLAS WILDERNESS

Deadwood Lakes

To Yakima

410

Rainier Fork American River

WENATCHEE NATIONAL FOREST

Yakima Peak

To Seattle

P

Tipsoo Lake

P

410

Naches Peak

N

0.2 mile
0.2 kilometer

have already been used; camp at least 100 feet from the lake; and use existing trails to get water, find a camp, and explore the shoreline.

If you're revitalized and you want more after your stint at the lake, continue around its eastern shoreline and head up to Sourdough Gap. The trail climbs steeply from the lake but soon mellows out as it snakes its way through open meadows. At 2.5 miles, you enter a stand of alpine firs where a small U-shaped spur trail branches off to the right and provides your first glimpse of Mount Adams and the snowcapped peaks of Goat Rocks Wilderness. Don't worry if you miss the trail; the views open in 0.25 mile, affording vistas of Mount Adams once again.

While the views in the distance are impressive, those immediately in front of you are just as noteworthy. The ridgeline is composed of pillars in shades of deep black and gray, which contrast sharply with the surrounding greenery. The trail rises to run below the ridge as it heads toward the pass. Just after the 3-mile mark, the trail crosses a scree slope that pours out from one of the columns above. Almost immediately after you cross this slope, you catch a quick glimpse of Mount Rainier through a gap in the ridgeline to the west. Pay close attention because the view is brief and easy to miss.

You reach Sourdough Gap at 3.2 miles. You have a couple of options from this point, the first a short jaunt over to the Mount Rainier National Park boundary. (If you decide to enter the park boundary, be aware that pets and firearms are prohibited.) Continue north from the gap, and you'll soon come to a junction; continue north across a scree slope to a small pass. Beyond the pass, you quickly reach the park boundary and begin a steep

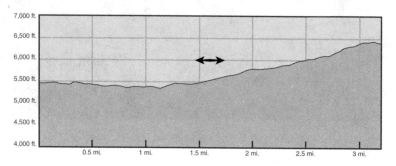

Magenta paintbrush adds a splash of color to an already dramatic landscape as you approach Sourdough Gap.

descent along an unmaintained trail to the aptly named Crystal Lake. For those hikers looking for a less adventurous outing, a small knoll just below the pass provides stunning views of Mount Rainier. Make sure to bring your camera to appreciate this photographers' playground.

If you want to do a long hike with a couple of friends, the second option is a thru-hike to Crystal Mountain Resort, a popular ski area. From the gap, continue northeast along the PCT to Bear Gap (3.3 miles). From here, follow the directions from Bear Gap in the description for the next hike (the total distance is approximately 9 miles from Chinook Pass).

PERMIT INFORMATION Northwest Forest Pass ($30/year) required; see tinyurl.com/northwestforestpass for more information. A backcountry permit is required at Crystal Lake; make reservations (see nps.gov/mora/planyourvisit/wilderness-permit.htm for details) or register in person at the White River Wilderness Information Center (360-569-6670) during operating hours. Self-issued permit available at trailhead for Sheep Lake.

DIRECTIONS

FROM SEATTLE: From I-405 just east of I-5, drive 2 miles east to WA 167; then drive 20 miles south to WA 410. Follow WA 410 east for 42 miles to the entrance of Mount Rainier National Park. Drive 18 miles past the park entrance and, just before WA 410 meets WA 123, bear left (east) to stay on WA 410. Drive 3.7 miles to Chinook Pass, and park in the large lot on the left (west) side of the road.

FROM TACOMA: From WA 512 just east of I-5, drive 14 miles east to WA 167. Bear right and, in 1 mile, turn right on WA 167. Drive 20 miles south to WA 410, and follow the remaining directions above.

FROM YAKIMA: From US 12 just west of I-82, drive 17 miles west. Where US 12 heads south at the T, continue west for 46 miles on WA 410 to Chinook Pass. Park in the large lot on your right.

GPS TRAILHEAD COORDINATES N46° 52.572' W121° 31.087'

12 Bullion Basin to Silver Creek

SCENERY: 🏠 🏠 🏠 🏠 🏠   TRAIL CONDITION: 🏠 🏠 🏠

CHILDREN: 🏠 🏠   DIFFICULTY: 🏠 🏠 🏠 🏠

SOLITUDE: 🏠 🏠 🏠 🏠   DISTANCE: 7 miles

HIKING TIME: 3–4 hours   GREEN TRAILS MAP: *Mount Rainier East 270*

OUTSTANDING FEATURES: Solitude, exceptional views of Mount Rainier, and myriad trails to keep you busy for as long as you like

I TEND TO AVOID WEEKEND CROWDS whenever possible, but there are times when getting out on a weekday just isn't possible. That's why I was so excited to find this relatively unknown loop at a popular ski resort: the scenery is breathtaking, the trails are quiet, and the hiking options are endless. Make sure that you bring a map—even the most experienced hikers are bound to make a wrong turn at one of the many junctions without one.

Descending from Blue Bell Pass to Crown Point

🚶🚶 From Parking Lot A at Crystal Mountain Resort, look for the trailhead sign for Bullion Basin near the chapel. Climb northwest away from the ski lodge up a steep dirt access road. In a few hundred feet, you'll arrive at the trailhead. Follow the trail for 0.4 miles, crossing Forest Road 410 a couple of times. After the second crossing, you'll arrive at the old trailhead for Bullion Basin (described in the first edition of this book), located near a pullout on the road.

Before you continue along the trail, take note of Silver Creek Trail 1192, your exit route on your right. The trail heading toward Bullion Basin is steep and dusty for the first 0.25 mile—a sign of the horsepackers who frequent this section—and crosses the road a couple of times before arriving at a clearing that looks out toward the ski area.

After a couple of switchbacks, the trail makes its way up the creek, and at 0.6 mile, a spur trail leads down to the water. This is a good spot to let thirsty dogs grab a drink before continuing up the trail; there's no more easily accessible water until you reach the basin.

At 1 mile, the real beauty of this hike begins as the trail alternates between lush meadows and mature, healthy stands of fir and hemlock. At 1.2 miles, the trail opens, and Mount Rainier can be seen to the southwest, providing a stunning backdrop to the slopes of the ski area. In 0.25 mile, you reach Bullion Basin, a large meadow with meandering streams that weave through the tall grass. As you enter the meadow, notice a steep, rugged path to the east that heads out of the basin and up toward the ridge to the Pacific Crest Trail (PCT). To help prevent erosion, continue on the main trail the short distance to Blue Bell Pass and the intersection with the PCT. Once you have crossed the meadow, you pass a large campsite with a couple of hitching posts. If you plan to camp here, be prepared to share with horses.

Just past the campsite, cross the creek as the trail climbs out of the basin to head south. At 1.8 miles is the first of three steep switchbacks that round the shoulder of the ridge. It may feel as if you're topping out at a pass, but you still have 0.4 miles to go. This is, however, a fantastic location to stop for lunch or a light snack. Rainier dominates the skyline, and steep slopes of sub-alpine daisies and lupine extend from the ridge into the valley below. After a short break, continue climbing on the west side of the ridge as you make your

Bullion Basin to Silver Creek

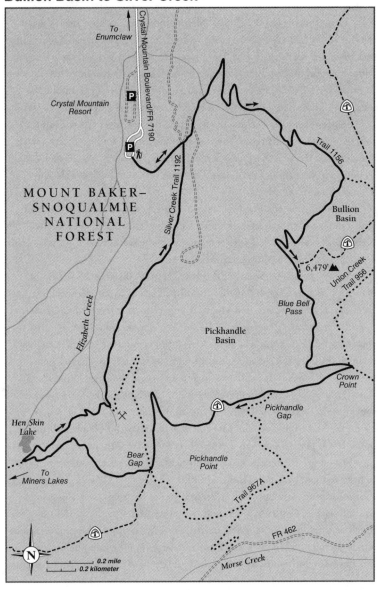

To Enumclaw

Crystal Mountain Boulevard/FR 7190

P

Crystal Mountain Resort

P

Silver Creek Trail 1192

Trail 1156

MOUNT BAKER–SNOQUALMIE NATIONAL FOREST

Bullion Basin

6,479'

Union Creek Trail 956

Blue Bell Pass

Elizabeth Creek

Pickhandle Basin

Crown Point

Pickhandle Gap

Hen Skin Lake

Bear Gap

Pickhandle Point

To Miners Lakes

Trail 967A

FR 462

Morse Creek

N

0.2 mile

0.2 kilometer

way toward the PCT. To the north, the PCT teeters along the ridgeline en route to Scout Pass and Norse Peak, a great out-and-back hike.

For those interested in continuing, head south on the PCT. In a few hundred feet, you reach Blue Bell Pass (6,300'), which sits between Summit 6479 and Crown Point. The hike from the pass to Crown Point is not for the faint of heart. The trail is narrow and exposed, with steep, sweeping views in every direction. As you round Crown Point, the angle eases off a bit as the trail makes a gradual eastern descent through a large, open meadow to the junction with Union Creek Trail 956. Continue southwest along the PCT as the trail makes one large switchback to Pickhandle Gap and the William O. Douglas Wilderness boundary.

At 3.2 miles, you reach the gap and yet another junction, this time with Trail 967A. The trail makes a stout ascent from Morse Creek, so don't be surprised to find fellow hikers out of breath and taking a well-earned break. From the gap, the trail rises slightly as it heads around Pickhandle Point. In 0.7 mile, the trail makes a long switchback to the south as it crosses a ridge and heads to the five-way junction of Bear Gap (5,880').

Even for the most experienced hikers, this is a confusing junction. Many of the signs are worn and lack maps. You have two options for getting back to the ski area: the first is to head north, traveling below the trail you just came in on; the second is to head west to Hen Skin Lake, which adds an extra mile or so to the hike but is more interesting.

If you decide to go to the lake, take the left of the two branches as you stand looking north from the junction. The trail gradually passes through

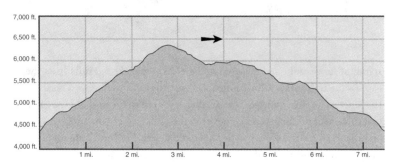

The quiet shores of Hen Skin Lake

stands of forest and open meadows and arrives at the lake 0.7 mile from the gap. As the trail makes a final switchback toward the shoreline, you reach the junction to Miners Lakes, two smaller lakes just to the west of Hen Skin. Continue around the lake's perimeter to the outlet, where the trail reaches an unmarked junction. Stay to the right and descend to Jim Town, an old mining camp next to Elizabeth Creek.

This final junction of the hike is relatively straightforward. Follow the signs for Silver Creek Trail 1192; the trail is fairly unremarkable until you pass a small tributary on a footbridge next to an old mine. Shortly after this, you travel beneath a ski lift and come out on a road that takes you back to FR 410 and the intersection with Bullion Basin Trail. From FR 410, retrace your steps back to Parking Lot A at Crystal Mountain Resort.

PERMIT INFORMATION Northwest Forest Pass ($30/year) required; see tinyurl.com/northwestforestpass for more information.

If you want to camp overnight at Crystal Mountain, current fees are $25 for nonelectric sites and $35 for electric sites. See crystal mountainresort.com/summer-planning/rv-parking for rules and information on nearby camping options outside the resort.

DIRECTIONS From the intersection of WA 410 and Roosevelt Avenue in Enumclaw, head east on WA 410 and, in about 34 miles, turn left at the sign for Crystal Mountain Resort onto Crystal Mountain Boulevard (FR 7190). Continue up the road for 6 miles to Crystal Mountain Resort, and follow the signs to Parking Lot A. Head toward the front of the lot, and look for the trailhead on the left. For additional directions from different starting points, see crystalmountain resort.com/summer-planning/summer-getting-here.

GPS TRAILHEAD COORDINATES N46° 56.255' W121° 28.142'

13 Big Crow Basin

SCENERY: ✿ ✿ ✿ ✿

CHILDREN: ✿ ✿

SOLITUDE: ✿ ✿ ✿

TRAIL CONDITION: ✿ ✿ ✿

DIFFICULTY: ✿ ✿ ✿ ✿

DISTANCE: 12.5 miles

HIKING TIME: 6–8 hours or overnight

GREEN TRAILS MAP: *Mount Rainier East 270*

OUTSTANDING FEATURES: Open meadows, a rickety old shelter, expansive views of numerous peaks, and a chance to glimpse mountain goats roaming the hills

THIS LOOP HIKE EXPLORES THE AMAZING subalpine terrain just north of Crystal Mountain Ski Area. While your jaunt on the Pacific Crest Trail (PCT) is a mere mile, the surrounding terrain is stunning. Make sure to bring plenty of water: sources are limited, and the trail can be hot and dry on a midsummer day.

🚶 From the trailhead, you immediately begin a steep, dusty hike up a series of relentless switchbacks. The occasional flutter of a flushed grouse

The remnants of a CCC shelter lie along the edge of Big Crow Basin.

and the cool shade of a silver fir forest make this section somewhat enjoyable, despite your having to trudge a consistent uphill grade. In just under 1 mile, the trail arrives at the old Norse Peak trail, which is now closed to restore areas that have been damaged by erosion. As you resume your hike along the main trail, you can see where people have cut switchbacks, eroding sections of the new trail. Please stay on the main path and resist taking shortcuts—they will abbreviate your hike by only a few seconds anyway.

As you continue to climb, the trail switchbacks a few more times before paralleling a drainage where you can occasionally catch glimpses south toward Crystal Mountain Ski Area. At 1.9 miles, the trail breaks out of the forest, and you can see the tip-top of Mount Rainier behind the ridgelines that spread from the summit of Crystal Mountain. This view is a teaser for what is to come.

The trail winds through open fields interspersed with small stands of evergreens for the next 0.5 mile before arriving at the junction for Goat Lake. Take note of this location—it's where you'll exit if you're interested in doing this hike as a loop. Remain on Trail 1191 as it makes one last, good uphill push. Rainier displays itself in all its glory 1 mile or so from the junction, allowing you to take a breather and enjoy the view.

Just a bit farther, you reach a narrow ridge that's forested on one side and open on the other. As you ascend, keep an eye out for an unmarked spur trail that branches to the left and descends into Big Crow Basin. The trail along the ridgeline eventually leads you to the summit of Norse Peak, elevation 6,856 feet, and the site of an old fire lookout erected in the 1930s and removed in 1956. Not much remains of the lookout; if you're feeling strong, however, the views are well worth the extra 1.4 miles.

If you're not feeling the call to summit Norse Peak, the wildflowers in the bowl below are just as stunning. The trail descends the ridge through a steep, loose section that mellows as you work around the upper part of the basin. Fields of flowers, including columbine, tiger lilies, valerian, and asters, hold your interest, and in less than 1 mile you'll be on the PCT.

From here, you have a couple of options. Those of you looking to get out overnight should head south on the PCT to a junction with Basin Lake Trail 987. The lake itself is less than 1 mile from the junction; however, it loses

Big Crow Basin

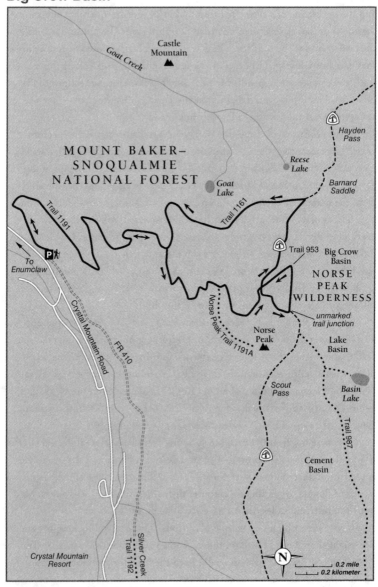

Castle Mountain

Goat Creek

MOUNT BAKER–
SNOQUALMIE
NATIONAL FOREST

Goat
Lake

Trail 1191

To
Enumclaw

Crystal Mountain Road

FR 410

Reese
Lake

Hayden
Pass

Barnard
Saddle

Trail 1161

Trail 953

Big Crow
Basin

NORSE
PEAK
WILDERNESS

unmarked
trail junction

Norse Peak Trail 1191A

Norse
Peak

Lake
Basin

Basin
Lake

Trail 987

Scout
Pass

Cement
Basin

Crystal Mountain
Resort

Silver Creek
Trail 1192

N

0.2 mile
0.2 kilometer

600 feet in elevation, making it somewhat of a bear to climb back out of. That said, the stunning turquoise waters in the shadow of a behemoth rock outcropping provide the ideal backcountry campsite and quickly make you forget the hike that awaits you in the morning.

If you're looking for something a little less ambitious, you can head east 0.25 miles on Crow Lake Way Trail 953. This short excursion brings you to an old, weathered shelter built by the Civilian Conservation Corps in the 1930s. While the structure's saggy frame and perforated roof may not provide much shelter these days, its location at the edge of Big Crow Basin's expansive meadow makes it anything but disappointing. A small stream nearby trickles year-round.

While exploring the area around the shelter, you may encounter a well-used path that takes off behind the hitching post and eventually leads you back to the PCT, but it's steep, and having to negotiate the loose rock means you won't save much time. To help prevent further erosion, retrace your steps on Trail 953.

Once you arrive back at the junction, head north on the PCT. The trail traverses a bowl and, in 0.5 mile, reaches Barnard Saddle. Continue along the ridge, and when you enter a stand of dense trees, keep an eye out for a signed junction to Cement Basin and take the unmarked trail that travels west toward Goat Lake. In less than 1 mile, you enter a spectacular basin where eroding pinnacles leave behind fields of talus slopes strewn with mountain goat paths. If you're lucky, you may see these impressive animals weaving their way through the cliff bands above.

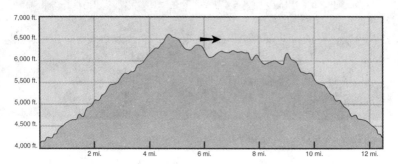

Goat Lake and the massive slopes that make up Castle Mountain

As you work your way across the bottom of the talus field, Goat Lake slowly comes into view. The trail travels well above the lake (which resembles more of a large pond); however, a series of game trails works its way down to the water's edge. More impressive than the lake itself is its backdrop, Castle Rock. This broad, massive rock formation across the valley rises sharply and will have you stumbling in your tracks.

From the basin, the trail ascends to a saddle, then climbs directly up a ridge to three hitching posts. As you gain the ridge, look for a trail off to the west that turns sharply south. This trail takes you back to Trail 1191, which is unmarked and easy to miss if you're not paying attention. If you reach the hitching posts, you have gone too far. As you descend, Rainier greets you once again, and the trail you came up on can be seen through gaps in the trees. You soon arrive back at Trail 1191, and in 2.5 miles, you're back at the trailhead. The small town of Greenwater is a short drive from the parking area and is the ticket for refueling a tired body.

PERMIT INFORMATION Northwest Forest Pass ($30/year) required; see tinyurl.com/northwestforestpass for more information.

DIRECTIONS From the intersection of WA 410 and Roosevelt Avenue in Enumclaw, head east on WA 410 and, in about 34 miles, turn left at the sign for Crystal Mountain Resort onto Crystal Mountain Boulevard (FR 7190). Continue up the road 4.2 miles, and turn left onto FR 410, which is marked by a brown metal sign and not to be confused with WA 410. The best place to park is at the large pullout at the beginning of the road. Walk 0.25 mile up FR 410 to the trailhead for Norse Peak, on the left side of the road.

GPS TRAILHEAD COORDINATES N46° 57.726' W121° 28.815'

14 Mirror Lake

SCENERY: ✿ ✿ ✿	TRAIL CONDITION: ✿ ✿ ✿ ✿
CHILDREN: ✿ ✿ ✿ ✿	DIFFICULTY: ✿ ✿
SOLITUDE: ✿ ✿	DISTANCE: 6 MILES
HIKING TIME: 4–5 hours	GREEN TRAILS MAP: Snoqualmie Pass 207

OUTSTANDING FEATURES: A gorgeous alpine lake that reflects Tinkham Peak's craggy outline, a couple of peaks for summit-hungry folks to scramble up, and a good day hike or overnight trip for kids

HIKING OPTIONS ABOUND along this corridor, mainly because of the extensive logging road system that surrounds it. Mirror Lake, for example, can be approached on the Pacific Crest Trail (PCT) from the north or the south. Although the southern approach is shorter, the trail lies in a clear-cut, and you end up spending more time in the car than out in the woods. To ensure that you make the most of your visit, I've listed a few hiking alternatives.

Mirror Lake lies in the shadow of Tinkham Peak.

🏃🏃 This hike is a true Washington treasure. Surrounded by a patchwork of logged slopes, the trail lies within the protective boundaries of an area that the U.S. Forest Service obtained in 2000 in hopes of preserving and rehabilitating a healthy forest along the Central Cascade crest.

To begin, head south on the PCT through an old clear-cut that immediately reminds you how fortunate we are that this area has been saved. For the first 0.25 mile, the trail is devoid of trees but thick with huckleberry bushes. It isn't uncommon to see a few people in the field in late summer or early fall with buckets in their hands and purplish-blue stains on their lips. Beyond the opening, the trail enters a thriving forest and crosses a few trickling creeks. Within the first mile, views open to the east, toward the deep-blue waters of the large Keechelus Lake and the fairly murky waters of the much smaller Twin Lakes.

In 0.5 mile, the trail enters a meadow at the base of Silver Peak, a popular springtime scramble that can be approached from the PCT via Olallie Meadow or from the more standard route along the ridgelines that fall toward Annette Lake on the peak's western side. Continuing along the trail, you reach Tinkham Peak, another popular scramble, southeast of Silver. Ambitious hikers have been known to tackle Tinkham, Silver, and Abiel (directly south of Silver) in a single day.

Remaining on the well-maintained trail, descend a couple of switchbacks, cross a small boulder field, and make a short climb to a bench near some watering holes. The trail can be mucky through this section, but the view of Tinkham should distract you from the suctioning sound your boots are making. From here, the trail continues its ever-gradual ascent across a mixture of forested slopes and open hillsides to arrive at a broad pass in 2.8 miles.

To make a loop out of this hike, head down Cold Creek Trail 1303 toward Twin Lakes. Before doing so, however, descend a quick 0.5 mile to Mirror Lake along the PCT.

From the saddle, the Mirror Lake Trail winds down a couple switchbacks, losing 300 feet in 0.5 mile, with views of Cottonwood Lake to the east (left). Like most of the lakes in this area, Cottonwood has a much shorter approach via a 1.1-mile excursion on Trail 1302 (leaving from Forest Road 5480). The PCT

Mirror Lake

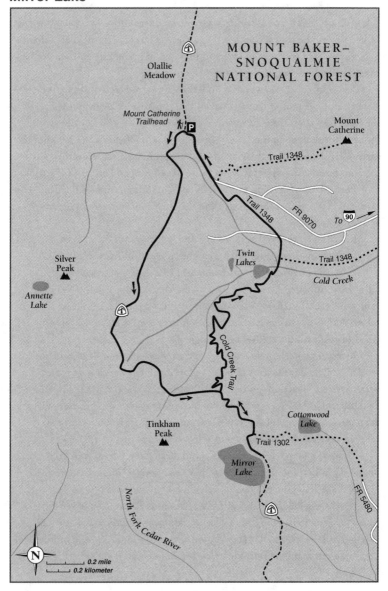

intersects this trail just before you reach Mirror Lake, so if you're feeling energetic, you can add 1 mile by hiking out and back to Cottonwood.

As you approach Mirror Lake, don't be surprised by the crowds along its shoreline. Many hikers approach it on the much shorter (and less interesting) Mirror Lake Trail, which joins the PCT as it approaches from the south. Both trails skirt the east side of the lake, where Tinkham's reflection can be seen in the placid, blue water. Those interested in sleeping outside will find campsites scattered throughout the area.

To make this hike a loop, reverse your course back to the junction with Cold Creek Trail 1303. This route is recommended only for experienced hikers and should not be attempted with children. The trail to Twin Lakes is steep (losing 1,400 feet in 1.7 miles), brushy, and can be slick as slime if there's any moisture in the air. On a positive note, you're almost guaranteed solitude all the way to the lake.

As you leave the saddle, the trail descends tight switchbacks on a somewhat slanted trail, where roots conspire to trip you. In 1 mile the trail crosses a large boulder field lined with devil's club, alders, and brambles. As you reach the valley floor, the trail skirts the south side of the lake, passing through a section of head-high brush to eventually spit you out at the outlet. Cross the notched log to access the lake's peaceful shores.

You may notice a faint footpath that cuts through the tall grass and marshy meadows and travels around most of the lake. Exploring the area, you may have trouble finding the second of the Twin Lakes: it's not you . . . the second lake has shrunk over time and resembles more of a large meadow these days.

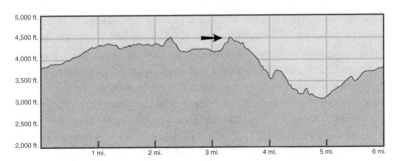

Early conditions can sometimes require clambering up and over blowdowns. This one was easy enough to negotiate on the hike into Mirror Lake.

Back on the trail, you pass a couple of nice campsites along a creek that drains from the lake. The trail soon joins Mount Catherine Trail 1348. From here, Cold Creek Trail, which you were on, heads east to end 0.8 mile ahead, at FR 9070. If you're tired of traveling on rugged trails, take this trail to the road and walk back to your car at Windy Pass. This option adds a couple miles to your hike and gains about the same elevation as the Mount Catherine Trail.

If you're ready to get the hike over with, continue on the rarely frequented Mount Catherine Trail. The trail soon crosses a U.S. Forest Service road. Don't confuse this with FR 9070, and make sure you pick up the trail on the far side of the road. From here, the trail climbs steeply along the east side of a brushy creek. The trail is overgrown and mucky in places, but the going is easier than on Cold Creek. Six hundred feet farther (approximately 1 mile from Twin Lakes), you reach FR 9070 at an obscure, unmarked trailhead. Turn left, and head uphill 0.25 mile back to your car. The total loop distance is 6 miles, not including the side trip to Mirror Lake.

PERMIT INFORMATION Northwest Forest Pass ($30/year) required; see tinyurl.com/northwestforestpass for more information.

DIRECTIONS Drive I-90 to Snoqualmie Pass (about 50 miles east of Seattle); get off at Hyak, Exit 54, and turn right (south) onto Hyak Drive. Go straight through a double stop sign—two stop signs stacked on top of each other. Just before you reach the ski-area parking lot, follow Hyak Drive as it curves left, back toward the interstate. The road quickly veers right and continues through a housing development. Ignore the DEAD END sign and continue driving, entering a gate and passing a sewage-treatment plant on the left side of the road at 0.5 mile. Just beyond, the road becomes gravel. You're now on FR 9070, a little more than a mile from the interstate.

In another 1.1 mile, bear right at the intersection to continue west along Cold Creek on FR 9070. About 1 mile farther, the road passes the Cold Creek Trailhead (barely visible from the road) at a hairpin turn. Continue driving to an obvious clear-cut, and you'll soon reach Windy Pass. Keep an eye out for the Mount Catherine Trailhead, which is on the left (south) side of the road, 5 miles from the double stop sign. Drive slowly and watch for cyclists in this designated mountain biking area.

GPS TRAILHEAD COORDINATES N47° 22.389' W121° 26.816'

15 Commonwealth Basin to Red Pass

SCENERY: ✿ ✿ ✿ ✿   TRAIL CONDITION: ✿ ✿ ✿ ✿

CHILDREN: ✿ ✿ ✿ ✿   DIFFICULTY: ✿ ✿ ✿

SOLITUDE: ✿ ✿ ✿   DISTANCE: 10 miles

HIKING TIME: 5 hours   GREEN TRAILS MAP: *Snoqualmie Pass 207*

OUTSTANDING FEATURES: Steep hills, dramatic views, parkland meadows, and abundant blueberries

THIS IS ONE OF THE MORE SPECTACULAR hikes in the Snoqualmie Pass area. Proximity to Seattle makes it an ideal destination if you want to slip away for a day or just a long afternoon. This trail has lots to engage children's interest and plenty of convenient turnaround spots if they get tired. Be aware that the last 0.25 mile (from the ridgecrest) is somewhat exposed.

Mount Thomson dominates the foreground from Red Pass.

🚶🚶 This hike starts out heading north along the Pacific Crest Trail (PCT). The trail gradually climbs through an old-growth forest of fir and hemlock, a good distraction from the I-90 corridor traffic. The sound of speeding cars is soon replaced by the gurgle of creeks and the chirping of songbirds as the trail wraps around a ridge and enters Alpine Lakes Wilderness.

After 2.5 miles, the trail reaches a junction. The PCT continues climbing toward Kendall Ridge, while Commonwealth Basin Trail branches to the left and gradually descends into an open meadow. Meandering streams, small stands of trees, pockets of wildflowers, and creekside campsites are just a few of the treasures to look forward to.

After 4 miles, you cross Commonwealth Creek, which is usually dry by mid- to late summer. Earlier in the season, you can easily wade through the shallow water or cautiously rock-hop across.

Once you cross the creek, the real climb begins. Tight, short switchbacks follow a narrow ridge for 500 feet, making this a steep ascent. However, you're rewarded with an amazing view about halfway up the ridge, with Guye Peak, Cave Ridge, and Alpental Ski Area to the southwest, and the broad slopes of Snoqualmie Mountain to the northwest. This spot is also the perfect place to catch your breath and take in some of the seasonal riches of this area, such as June's trilliums, whose colors range from white to violet; July's bright-red scarlet paintbrush; and August's bumper crop of blueberries.

The trail's grade gradually eases as it approaches Red Pond, a good spot to rest on a boulder on a lazy afternoon. From here, you also have a great view of the deep-red, rocky slopes of Red Mountain. For those continuing on to the pass, take the second spur trail that you passed as you approached the pond on your way up. The trail makes a couple of long switchbacks before traveling through open talus slopes on its course approximately 200 feet above the pond. If you're doing this hike early in the season, be aware that snow lingers on this west-facing slope, which can make the trail difficult to follow and easy to slip on.

After a long ascent, the trail enters a stand of subalpine firs and switchbacks to the crest of the ridge, where you get stunning views of the valley and

Commonwealth Basin to Red Pass

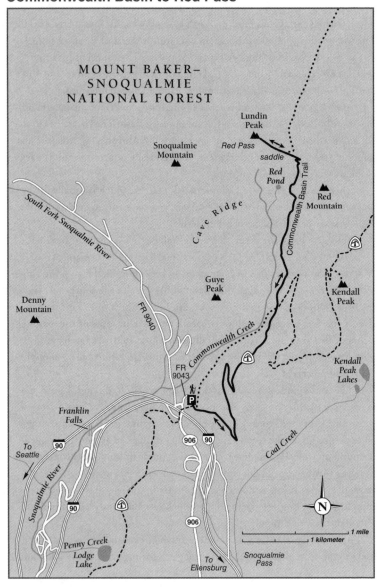

MOUNT BAKER–
SNOQUALMIE
NATIONAL FOREST

Lundin
Peak

Snoqualmie
Mountain

Red Pass

saddle

Red
Pond

Red
Mountain

C a v e   R i d g e

Commonwealth Basin Trail

South Fork Snoqualmie River

Guye
Peak

Kendall
Peak

Denny
Mountain

FR 9040

Commonwealth Creek

FR
9043

Kendall
Peak
Lakes

Franklin
Falls

P

906

90

To
Seattle

Snoqualmie River

90

Coal Creek

Penny Creek
Lodge
Lake

906

To
Ellensburg

Snoqualmie
Pass

N

1 mile

1 kilometer

a sea of peaks beyond. Follow the trail as it descends slightly to a short series of switchbacks to Red Pass (5,350').

If you're looking for a good lunch spot with a breathtaking view, a few side trails branch north off the main trail, just before you reach the pass. Try to take the most-used path, which ascends 100 feet to a high point. From there, the views to the north are dramatic, to say the least, with steep, rocky slopes and cascading creeks tumbling toward the deep gorges of the Middle Fork of the Snoqualmie River. Mount Thomson dominates the view to the northeast, its massive form jutting out from a series of craggy ridgelines and imposing peaks. The Snoqualmie Ski Area, resembling a tiny village that might be found somewhere in the Alps, is visible to the south.

If you're feeling adventurous, an unmaintained trail leads to the summit of Lundin Peak (6,057'). The "trail," which is really more of a climber's path, heads east from Red Pass and ascends steeply through benches of heather and small rock outcroppings. The summit is 0.5 mile up, and if your heart isn't already pumping, it will be when you peek over the edge at the vertical drop off the northwest side of the peak. The views from this craggy perch are well worth the extra effort, with Snoqualmie Mountain's broad slopes to the west and Lake Keechelus's long, narrow shorelines to the south. Although this trail is relatively well traveled, it's really more of a scramble than a hike; bring an ice axe early in the season.

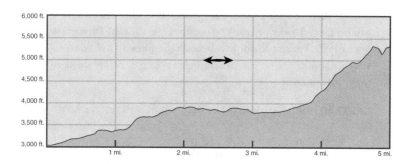

Looking down at Red Pond on the climb to Red Pass

PERMIT INFORMATION Northwest Forest Pass ($30/year) required; see tinyurl.com/northwestforestpass for more information. Self-issued permits available at the trailhead.

DIRECTIONS Follow I-90 to Snoqualmie Pass, and take Exit 52 if coming from the west or Exit 53 if coming from the east. Turn north onto Alpental Access Road, pass beneath the freeway, and immediately turn onto the spur road branching to the right. Follow the signs to the PCT parking area.

GPS TRAILHEAD COORDINATES N47° 25.668' W121° 24.807'

16 Kendall Katwalk

SCENERY: ✿ ✿ ✿ ✿	TRAIL CONDITION: ✿ ✿ ✿ ✿
CHILDREN: ✿ ✿	DIFFICULTY: ✿ ✿ ✿
SOLITUDE: ✿	DISTANCE: 12 miles
HIKING TIME: 6 hours	GREEN TRAILS MAP: *Snoqualmie Pass 207*

OUTSTANDING FEATURES: Airy views, flower-filled gardens, and a hike that's on the PCT the entire time

THIS TRAIL IS NEW for the second edition of this book. When I was deciding on a hike from Snoqualmie Pass to include in the first edition, I chose Commonwealth Basin (see previous hike). Once the book was released, I had numerous people ask why I never made it to the Kendall Katwalk. When it came time for the second edition, I decided to give this hike a try. As the trail took me higher and higher into the subalpine, I quickly came to realize what all the hype was about, and the precarious views from the Katwalk were like icing on a cake.

Before I begin, I should mention that this is one of the more popular hikes in this book and appeals to myriad groups: ultradistance runners, horsepackers, day hikers, mushroom hunters, berry pickers, Pacific Crest Trail (PCT) enthusiasts, thru-hikers . . . need I go on? Its close proximity to Seattle and dramatic views are the perfect recipe for drawing a crowd. That said, don't let this trail's popularity dissuade you. You may just want to save this little gem for a weekday excursion.

From the parking lot, head north on the PCT. In a short distance, the trail passes a picnic table then comes to a T. Stay right; the left branch is just a side trail to the upper parking lot. A bit farther, the trail passes an abandoned gravel trail. This was known as the Commonwealth Creek Trail and was part of the old Cascade Crest Trail, the established high route through Washington before the PCT.

Remain on the main trail; in just over 2 miles, it enters the Alpine Lakes Wilderness Area. In 2.5 miles, the trail passes the turnoff for Commonwealth Basin (Hike 15). Continue heading north on the PCT, passing through

Kendall Katwalk

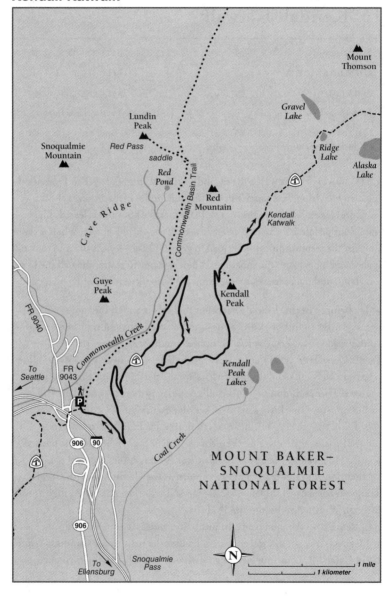

Mount Thomson

Gravel Lake

Ridge Lake

Alaska Lake

Lundin Peak

Snoqualmie Mountain

Red Pass

saddle

Red Pond

Kendall Katwalk

Red Mountain

Cave Ridge

Commonwealth Basin Trail

Guye Peak

Kendall Peak

Commonwealth Creek

FR 9040

To Seattle

FR 9043

P

Kendall Peak Lakes

906

90

Coal Creek

MOUNT BAKER–
SNOQUALMIE
NATIONAL FOREST

906

To Ellensburg

Snoqualmie Pass

N

1 mile

1 kilometer

a slide path with great views up toward Red Mountain and the Commonwealth Basin. Just beyond the path, the trail rounds a switchback and turns south, heading back into the cool shade of the forest.

At 3.3 miles, the trail crosses a creek and soon after enters another large slide path; evidence of its power can be seen by the massive pile of fallen trees in the basin below. The trail can be a little tricky in this section if you aren't paying attention. Keep your eye out for the trail to make a sharp right back into the brush when you begin to climb up a series of large rocks. This is an excellent place to gorge yourself on huckleberries, so take your time when navigating through this section.

From the slide path, the trail reenters the forest and quickly comes to a small campsite. At 3.8 miles, the trail rounds another switchback and turns east, working its way toward a forested saddle at 4,700 feet. There's a spot for a single tent, but views are limited, and there is no water.

As you leave the saddle, the trail turns north and begins a steady climb into the subalpine. If you've been impressed with the views up until this point, they are only going to get better. The trail travels along the west flank of Kendall Peak (5,784'), crosses a talus slope, and after a couple more switchbacks comes to a dazzling field of wildflowers known as Kendall Gardens. Distant views of Mount Rainier can be seen to the south, with Lundin Peak and Red Mountain looming much closer to the north.

Continuing on, the trail traverses high above a couple of small tarns then rounds the north shoulder of Kendall Peak. From the saddle,

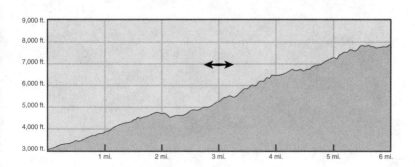

a climber's trail can be found east of the ridge. The path ascends the north shoulder of Kendall Peak and involves Class 3–4 climbing. If the summit seems a bit daunting, just heading up the climber's trail a short ways provides great views and a more secluded spot to take a break.

Continuing along the PCT, the trail heads northeast and in just under a half mile reaches the Katwalk. A warning sign for equestrians to dismount is the first indication that you have arrived. For those who start to sweat when they hear the word "exposure," a large, flat area just before the Katwalk begins makes for a great place to soak in the views. With that said, the trail is wide and the Katwalk is impressive, as it was literally blasted out of the granite. Views north into the Alpine Lakes Wilderness are stunning, with Mount Thomson (6,554') being one of the more prominent land features.

If you're looking to extend your hike or are interested in staying out for a night, it's another 1.5 miles down to Gravel and Ridge Lakes. Camping is available just off the western shore of Gravel Lake but is prohibited at Ridge. This is an extremely popular destination for backpackers and thru-hikers, so try to head out midweek if hiking during peak season. If you've had your fill of alpine views, simply turn south and head back down the PCT.

PERMIT INFORMATION Northwest Forest Pass ($30/year) required; see tinyurl.com/northwestforestpass for more information. Self-issued permits available at the trailhead.

DIRECTIONS Follow I-90 to Snoqualmie Pass, and take Exit 52 if coming from the west and Exit 53 if you're coming from the east. Turn north onto Alpental Access Road, pass beneath the freeway, and immediately turn onto the spur road branching to the right. Follow the signs to the PCT parking area.

GPS TRAILHEAD COORDINATES N47° 25.668' W121° 24.807'

OPPOSITE: *A dramatic view from Kendall Katwalk*

17 Spectacle Lake

SCENERY: ✿ ✿ ✿ ✿	TRAIL CONDITION: ✿ ✿ ✿
CHILDREN: ✿ ✿ ✿ ✿ ✿ *(to Pete Lake)*	DIFFICULTY: ✿ ✿ ✿
SOLITUDE: ✿ ✿ ✿	DISTANCE: 20 miles

HIKING TIME: 2–3 days

GREEN TRAILS MAPS: *Kachess Lake 208 and Snoqualmie Pass 207*

OUTSTANDING FEATURES: An old-growth forest; a great first lake to take kids on an overnight; and, for those willing to put in a little extra effort, a glacier-carved lake encircled by jagged peaks

THIS HIKE IS BROKEN INTO TWO very different legs. The first leg takes you to a peaceful little lake called Pete. Mostly flat and heavily used by horsepackers and hikers alike, this is great for beginning backpackers or families with kids. The second leg gains 1,300 feet (most of that in the last few miles) on its way to the secluded, glacier-polished shores of Spectacle Lake.

Crossing the Delate Falls footbridge just below Spectacle Lake

This hiker-only lake offers excellent mountain views and is more than worth the additional exertion.

🏃🏃 This hike begins in a tranquil setting at the far northwest corner of Cooper Lake. From the trailhead, Pete Lake Trail 1323 gently rolls through stands of old-growth Douglas-fir and hemlock, paralleling Cooper River, which for much of the hike cannot be seen or heard. The trail gains a mere 300 feet on its 4.5-mile journey to Pete Lake, making it a great destination for those with kids.

As you leave the trailhead (2,800'), take note of the crystal-clear pools of the Cooper River. The trail quickly strays from the slow-moving water and enters the cool shade of the forest canopy. At 1.4 miles, the trail meets up with Tired Creek Trail 1317, which branches to the northeast en route to Waptus Lake. Remain on Pete Lake Trail, and in another 0.5 mile, enter Alpine Lakes Wilderness.

At 3.1 miles, a campsite lies just off the trail if you're looking to escape the crowds for a night. Beyond the site, the trail turns away from the river, passes a meadow, and, in another mile, crosses a couple of rocky side streams that are usually dry by late summer or fall. A leisurely 4.5 miles later, you arrive at Pete Lake, elevation 2,980 feet.

This forested little lake is hard to beat in terms of accessibility, and the views into the Lemah Range create an alpinelike environment, without requiring you to climb quite that high. It's not nearly as breathtaking or secluded as Spectacle Lake, but it's a great option if you don't want to schlep your pack another 1,300 feet to Spectacle. Either way, it's the perfect spot to enjoy lunch while contemplating your next move.

If you decide to continue (which I highly recommend), hike around the north side of the lake, bypassing the turnoff for Escondido Lake and Waptus Pass. As you leave the lake's shrubby shoreline, the trail turns west and begins a 2-mile ascent of the Lemah Creek drainage before arriving at a nice creek-side camp tucked in a stand of trees.

If water is low and the crossing looks safe, wade or rock-hop your way across Lemah Creek at the well-signed crossing, and continue another 0.8 mile to the Pacific Crest Trail (PCT). If the water is high, continue along

Spectacle Lake

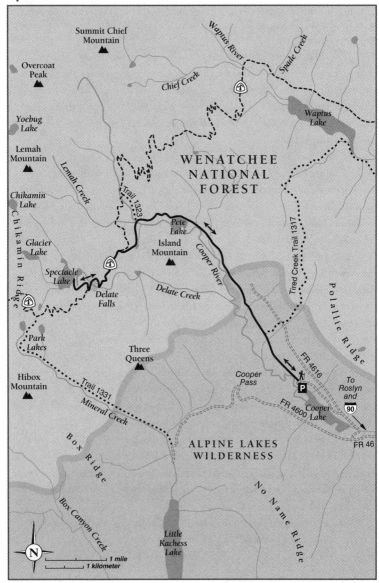

Lemah Meadow Trail 1323B to the PCT and cross the creek on a footbridge, adding 1 mile in each direction to your hike.

The PCT remains forested and fairly flat for the next 0.5 mile. Glancing eastward, you catch glimpses of Delate Meadows, motivating you on your climb into the high country. Long, somewhat relentless switchbacks wind back and forth, offering occasional views of Chikamin Ridge and Three Queens Mountain (6,687').

Just before you reach the 9-mile mark, the trail reaches Delate Falls, a spectacular place to take a well-earned break. From here, you have two alternatives for getting to Spectacle Lake. The first is to ascend a hard-to-find and overgrown shortcut known as "The Staircase." The trail heads right just after the last switchback before the Delate Falls footbridge and is really more of a root-and-rock scramble. But it cuts 0.5 mile from the hike and rewards you with another waterfall that pours from the outlet at the eastern end of the lake.

If you're carrying a big pack or the trail is slick, feel free to take the much mellower PCT another mile past the footbridge to the second turnoff for Spectacle Lake. This option adds about 100 feet of elevation gain but is more likely to get you there without any hitches. Descend to the lake along a hiker-only trail that's fairly steep and rutted, passing granite outcroppings scattered through fields of huckleberry bushes and squatty evergreens.

Arriving at Spectacle Lake (4,239'), you'll most likely forget the pain in your legs and the kink in your neck as you gaze out at the crystal-clear waters that seem to extend in every direction toward the mighty peaks that surround it. A maze of social trails guides you across glacier-polished rock to a finger

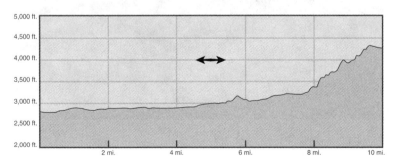

Strolling in to Pete Lake

of land that juts out on the south side of the lake. Excellent campsites can be found throughout this area, but like all alpine treasures, the vegetation is fragile, so please do your part to preserve it.

Views from this camp are anything but disappointing. The longest arm of the lake stretches north toward the spires, mini-arêtes, and hanging glaciers that make up Lemah Peak, the most dramatically aesthetic peak in the cirque. Southwest of Lemah is Chikamin Peak, and south of that extends rugged Chikamin Ridge. Glacier and Chikamin Lakes lie west and north of Spectacle, further evidence of the retreating glaciers that carved out this beautiful landscape.

If you have the time, spend more than one night in this area. One great approach is to spend your first night down low, either at Pete Lake or along Lemah Creek, then get an early start on your second day and set up camp at Spectacle Lake. If time and energy permit, a strong hiker can get back on the southbound PCT and day hike 4.5 miles farther, to Chikamin Pass (5,780'), where alpine vistas await. Even without hiking to Chikamin Pass, you'll want to spend as much time as possible soaking up the gorgeous high country that surrounds Spectacle Lake.

PERMIT INFORMATION Northwest Forest Pass ($30/year) required; see tinyurl.com/northwestforestpass for more information. Self-issued permits available at the trailhead.

DIRECTIONS From I-90, take Exit 80 toward Roslyn and Salmon La Sac. Turn left at the top of the off-ramp, follow the road 2.7 miles, and turn left at a T-junction onto WA 903 North. Drive through the town of Roslyn, following the signs for Salmon La Sac.

Follow WA 903 for 14.5 miles past Roslyn, and turn left onto Forest Road 46, following the signs for Cooper Lake. Cross the Cle Elum River and, in 4.7 miles, turn right onto FR 4616, signed PETE LAKE TRAIL. Cross the outlet bridge, turn left, and drive another 2 miles to the trailhead, at the northwest corner of Cooper Lake.

GPS TRAILHEAD COORDINATES N47° 26.051' W121° 11.223'

18 Cathedral and Deception Passes

SCENERY: ✿ ✿ ✿ ✿

CHILDREN: ✿ ✿ ✿ *(5 stars to Hyas Lake)*

SOLITUDE: ✿ ✿ ✿

HIKING TIME: 7 hours or 2 days

TRAIL CONDITION: ✿ ✿ ✿

DIFFICULTY: ✿ ✿ ✿ ✿

DISTANCE: 14.5 miles

GREEN TRAILS MAP: *Stevens Pass 176*

OUTSTANDING FEATURES: Steep creeks, rugged terrain, sparkling alpine lakes, and big, beautiful mountains

THIS LOOP HIKE CAN BE DONE in one somewhat strenuous day—but this is one of my favorite sections in Alpine Lakes Wilderness, and rushing through it would be regrettable. You have multiple backpacking options, including a couple of lakes that are great for novices or families wanting to bring along the kids.

🚶 The first 0.25 mile of the trail follows an abandoned road. A sturdy bridge provides access over the Cle Elum River and marks the start of the true

Fall foliage along a small tarn near Cathedral Pass

trail to Cathedral Pass. From here, the trail quickly enters the cool shade of the forest canopy, which can provide much-needed relief as you begin a moderate but steady climb toward Squaw Lake. In 0.5 mile, the trail crosses into Alpine Lakes Wilderness, where fires are prohibited above 5,000 feet and at the popular but fragile shores of Deep Lake (4,380').

Beyond the boundary, the trail resumes its ascent up lengthy switchbacks through a forest of sweet-smelling pines. In 2.1 miles, you reach the turnoff for Waptus and Michael Lakes along Trail Creek Trail 1322. Continue on Trail 1345 toward Squaw Lake and Cathedral Pass. Just beyond the junction, you leave the switchbacks behind as the trail begins a steep 0.25-mile climb straight up the hillside. At 2.4 miles, the trail flattens back out, allowing you to catch your breath and enjoy the next 0.25 mile to the lake.

The trail pops out in marshy meadows at Squaw Lake's northeast shoreline. With good picnicking spots and smaller crowds than at Hyas Lake, this is a great option for a mellow day hike: it's hard to go wrong relaxing at an alpine lake. Excellent tent-camping spots are set back from the lake's shoreline; there's also a designated pit toilet.

Continuing toward Cathedral Pass, the trail skirts the shoreline and passes a horse camp at the lake's inlet. From here, the trail begins another climb, crossing the inlet a couple of times along the way. As the trail rises above the lake, the terrain takes on a more rugged appearance, weaving around large boulders.

At 3.2 miles and 5,000 feet, another sign warns that fires are prohibited in the area. As you continue, you enter a subalpine region; the trees are shorter and the huckleberry bushes thicker, and clumps of heather cover the ground. The next mile takes you through gorgeous meadows and past small snowmelt ponds. Much of the trail is elevated on boardwalks to protect the delicate and sometimes soggy vegetation below.

Cathedral Pass (5,620') is 4.5 miles from the trailhead; here you meet up with the Pacific Crest Trail (PCT). The pass sits near the base of Cathedral Rock, a formidable peak that rises sharply from the parkland meadows surrounding it. The view from here is powerful, to say the least, so an out-and-back hike would be far from disappointing. There's also ample cross-country exploring to do from here, with lots of great camping. Making a day

Cathedral and Deception Passes

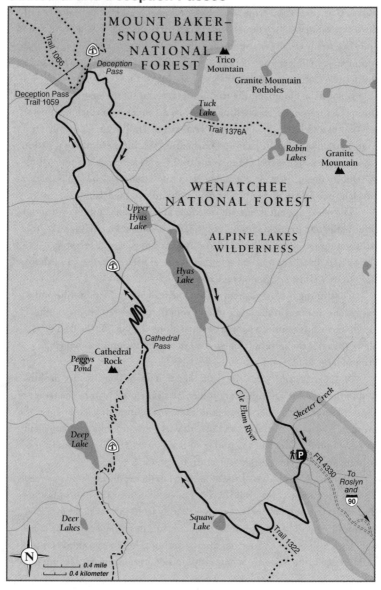

MOUNT BAKER–
SNOQUALMIE
NATIONAL
FOREST

Trail 1066

Deception
Pass

Deception Pass
Trail 1059

Trico
Mountain

Granite Mountain
Potholes

Tuck
Lake

Trail 1376A

Robin
Lakes

Granite
Mountain

WENATCHEE
NATIONAL FOREST

Upper
Hyas
Lake

ALPINE LAKES
WILDERNESS

Hyas
Lake

Cathedral
Pass

Peggys
Pond

Cathedral
Rock

Cle Elum River

Skeeter Creek

Deep
Lake

FR 4330

To
Roslyn
and
90

Deer
Lakes

Squaw
Lake

Trail 1322

N

0.4 mile
0.4 kilometer

hike—heading 3 miles from a camp at the pass to Deep Lake—would round out a wonderful three-day weekend.

To continue the loop to Deception Pass, turn north when you arrive at the PCT. If you decide on this option, be warned that two creeks pour from the icy slopes of Mount Daniel, and these can be treacherous to cross during times of peak snowmelt or heavy rain. Many backpackers have been forced to turn around at these creeks; check with the U.S. Forest Service if you're concerned about conditions.

As you descend from Cathedral Pass, the trail remains in the shadow of Cathedral Rock, its silhouette transforming as you wrap around its eastern flank. A narrow valley filled with car-sized boulders separates you from this daunting rock formation. The trail loses elevation quickly down tight switchbacks that wind through stands of hemlocks and swaths of huckleberries. Before you know it, you're back in the forest, making long, gentle switchbacks once again.

At 5.8 miles, the trail comes to a small clearing that provides a bird's-eye view of Hyas and Upper Hyas Lakes. The views come and go as you continue descending toward a large boulder field. At the toe of the boulders, two creeks converge; you'll find shady, creekside campsites here. Water can be somewhat sparse at the crossing in late summer or early fall, but just downstream from the sites is a year-round source.

The trail continues its descent downvalley through a hodgepodge of mountain hemlock, Douglas-fir, alder, and red cedar. Less than 1 mile from the first creek, you reach another. Beyond the crossing, the trail crosses

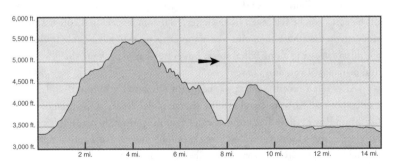

Views come and go as clouds swirl around the summit of Cathedral Peak.

numerous avalanche slide paths that can be overgrown and brushy. The magnitude of these slides is evidenced by the hundreds of trees littering the valley floor like matchsticks.

The trail soon reaches the first of two sketchy creek crossings. The power of the creek can be felt, even in low water, as it comes roaring through a rocky slot canyon just above the point where you cross it. You may be able to find a semisafe crossing along fallen trees; however, plan to get your shoes wet, and be happy if you don't have to.

After safely crossing the creek, begin the climb to Deception Pass. In 1 mile, the trail turns east and hits the second major creek, at the head of the Cle Elum River valley. The crossing can be nothing more than a simple rock hop late in the season; regardless, use caution because the rocks are slippery, and taking a spill this far from the trailhead would definitely ruin your day.

Beyond the creek, the trail keeps climbing, passing a small pond with a couple of campsites lacking views before reaching the broad, forested saddle known as Deception Pass (4,475'). From the pass, you have a few routes to choose from. The PCT continues its journey north-northeast, Marmot Lake Trail 1066 branches 3.5 miles to the west, and Deception Creek Trail 1059 goes north to US 2, ending about 6 miles outside the town of Skykomish.

To finish the loop, head down the Cle Elum River drainage along Trail 1376. As you descend, crazy assortments of colorful fungi pop up trailside. Avid mushroom hunters come from near and far to harvest these delectable treats during the peak picking season. Even if mushrooms aren't your area of expertise, their interesting shapes and slimy texture will fascinate you.

In a little more than 0.5 mile, the trail intersects the turnoff for Tuck and Robin Lakes. These alpine gems have been compared in beauty to those that lie in the heavily regulated Enchantment region. Because no permits are required, these lakes are in jeopardy of being loved to death. If you decide to explore this area (which I advise doing on a weekday), use preexisting camp-sites and social trails and bring a stove: campfires are prohibited.

Continuing on Trail 1376, a mile-long, knee-pounding descent brings you to the valley floor. You cross several small streams and rocky creeks en route to the swampy shoreline of Upper Hyas Lake. From here, you can see your entire route from Cathedral Rock to the head of the Cle Elum River, with immense Mount Daniel dominating the background. The camping around the lake is less than ideal, with a couple of horsey-smelling sites and muddy access to the water.

Just beyond the upper lake's outlet lies Hyas Lake. An easy 1.5 miles from the trailhead parking lot, this mile-long lake has abundant campsites (and pit toilets) for people looking to "get their feet wet" in the backpacking world. As you pass the sites, you can hear young kids splashing in the nearby water and novice backpackers saying things like, "I thought you brought the poles." The lake has the same stunning views as Upper Hyas, so it's no won-der these sites are packed. If you're looking for solitude, camp at any of the lakes mentioned earlier in the description.

Leaving the lake, the trail becomes a wide, heavily used path, a sign that the majority of the people in this area come to stay at Hyas Lakes. The ground is fairly level, making the last stretch of this 14.5-mile hike pleasant. Make sure to leave some time on the drive home to check out the town of Roslyn, made famous by the 1990s hit TV show *Northern Exposure*.

PERMIT INFORMATION Northwest Forest Pass ($30/year) required; see tinyurl.com/northwestforestpass for more information. Self-issued permits available at the trailhead.

DIRECTIONS From I-90, take Exit 80 toward Roslyn and Salmon La Sac. Turn left at the top of the off-ramp, follow the road 2.7 miles, and turn left at a T-junction onto WA 903 North. Drive through the town of Roslyn, following the signs for Salmon La Sac. The road forks 16.7 miles past Roslyn—veer right onto Forest Road 4330, toward Tucquala Lake. In 7.6 miles, you'll reach the Scatter Creek ford, which could present a problem in high water if you have a low-clearance vehicle. Continue past the ford another 5 miles to the road's end. Both trailheads are located in the large parking area.

GPS TRAILHEAD COORDINATES N47° 32.595' W121° 5.808'

Alpine vistas and stunning meadows are just a couple of the features that make Cathedral Pass such a memorable place.

19 Surprise and Glacier Lakes

SCENERY: ✿ ✿ ✿ ✿	TRAIL CONDITION: ✿ ✿ ✿ ✿
CHILDREN: ✿ ✿	DIFFICULTY: ✿ ✿ ✿
SOLITUDE: ✿ ✿	DISTANCE: 10 miles

HIKING TIME: 6–7 hours or overnight   GREEN TRAILS MAP: *Stevens Pass 176*

OUTSTANDING FEATURES: A creekside hike through a mossy forest, two alpine lakes, and spectacular views of surrounding peaks

THIS CLASSIC HIKE is accessible rain or shine. Even on a cold, drippy day, when the mountaintops are shrouded in mist, the forest takes on a mystical feel, with its moss-covered rocks, mushroom-speckled trees, and crystal-clear creek. Once you have ascended from the valley, you're rewarded with two splendid alpine lakes with great shoreline campsites. If you head out on a weekend, be prepared to share these gems with others—their proximity to Seattle makes them a hot destination.

As you begin this hike, you may wonder, "Where are all of those wonderful old-growth trees?" Don't worry—you'll see them soon enough. First you have to get up a steep, heart-pumping, rutted-out road; pass under enormous, buzzing power lines; and, in 0.25 mile, arrive at the official trailhead for Surprise Lake Trail 1060 (2,200').

The trail branches south off the road, immediately entering a thick forest full of monster hemlock, Douglas-fir, and cedar. A boardwalk keeps you above the waterlogged muck that makes up the forest floor, a sign of the massive amount of precipitation this area receives. You'll hear occasional whistle blasts from the train rolling through the valley, giving the hike an old-time feel.

In 0.5 mile, the trail reaches a snag dotted with slimy mushrooms, which marks the entrance into Alpine Lakes Wilderness. From here, the trail continues its gradual ascent, offering occasional glimpses into the crystal-clear, icy-cold waters of Surprise Creek. Cross it on a log at 1.2 miles to find excellent creekside campsites.

Surprise and Glacier Lakes

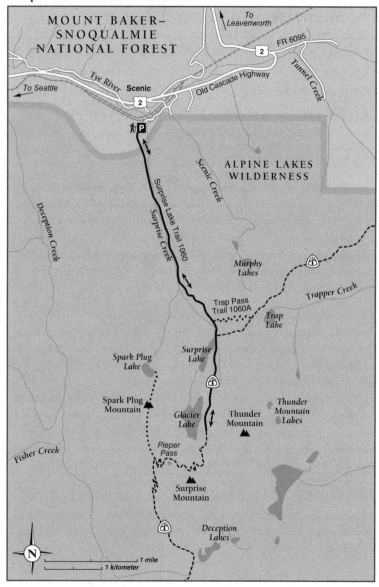

This next section takes you through a broad valley, where snow slides roar from steep slopes to the east and west of the drainage. Follow the trail past a large boulder with a mossy microforest sprouting from it. A bit farther, you cross the toe of an avalanche path, where large rocks sit among an entanglement of devil's club and slide alder.

At 1.6 miles, the trail arrives at another creekside camp. One site has room for two small tents. The trail sticks close to the creek for another 0.75 mile and then switchbacks up the east side of the valley. As you climb, vistas begin to open to the west, toward an unnamed cirque north of Spark Plug Mountain. You continue to climb for the next 2 miles before arriving at the creek once again. The trail parallels the boulder-choked waters for 0.5 mile before reaching a junction with Trap Pass Trail 1060A. This trail eventually grinds its way up to the Pacific Crest Trail (PCT), gaining 700 feet in 0.6 mile.

For those looking for a slightly easier path to the PCT, follow the signs to Surprise Lake. The trail crosses Surprise Creek on a confusing maze of social trails and soon arrives at the lake's northeast shore (4,508'). This is one of the more heavily used lakes in the area, so please camp at designated sites, and observe any closures or restoration efforts in the area. If you're out for the day, look for a wonderful picnic rock just off the trail that wraps around the east side of the lake.

From Surprise Lake, continue south as the trail rises away from the lakeshore. Follow a rib, and, in 0.5 mile, you arrive at the PCT. Continue south past a narrow pond and in less than 0.25 mile, the trail begins a traverse

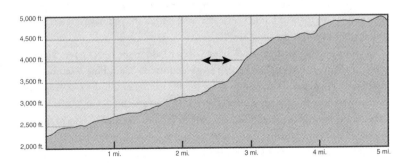

One of many huge boulders that line the trail to Surprise and Glacier Lakes

50–100 feet above the rockbound shores of Glacier Lake (4,806'). There's no official sign for the lake, so keep an eye out for a trail that branches to the west.

The deep-blue water of Glacier Lake, which lies in the shadow of Spark Plug Mountain (6,311'), is gorgeous, with great camping available among sparse trees on the east bank. Once you have settled in, you have a few options for further exploration.

Continue south on the PCT from Glacier Lake to the 6,000-foot Pieper Pass. From here, you can head north cross-country to Spark Plug Mountain and Spark Plug Lake, or continue along the PCT another 2 miles to Deception Lake. Extremely motivated, strong hikers can climb another 1.3 miles from the lakes to the top of Surprise Mountain (6,330'), where stunning views of the glaciated slopes of Mount Daniel await. When you have had your fill of this stunning country, retrace your route to the trailhead.

PERMIT INFORMATION Northwest Forest Pass ($30/year) required; see tinyurl.com/northwestforestpass for more information. Self-issued permits available at the trailhead.

DIRECTIONS From US 2 in Everett just east of I-5, drove east about 60 miles toward Stevens Pass. Continue 0.7 mile past milepost 58 to an unmarked road. Turn south toward the service center for Burlington Northern Railroad. Cross the railroad tracks and turn right. Continue another 0.1 mile, following a hiker sign to the trailhead. A steep, narrow road continues beyond the main parking area, but it's not worth getting your car stuck in an effort to avoid a mere 0.2 mile of walking.

GPS TRAILHEAD COORDINATES N47° 42.309′ W121° 9.411′

Mushrooms take root on a moss-covered stump.

SCENERY: ✿ ✿ ✿	TRAIL CONDITION: ✿ ✿ ✿
CHILDREN: ✿ ✿ ✿	DIFFICULTY: ✿ ✿ ✿
SOLITUDE: ✿ ✿ ✿	DISTANCE: 4 miles
HIKING TIME: 3 hours	GREEN TRAILS MAP: *Stevens Pass 176*

OUTSTANDING FEATURES: Quick, easy access to Alpine Lakes Wilderness, good huckleberry picking, and an opportunity to explore a variety of lakes scattered north and south along the PCT

THIS TRAIL'S PROXIMITY TO SEATTLE and relatively quick access into Alpine Lakes Wilderness made me wonder, "Where are all the people?" As I hit the trail, my thighs immediately began to burn. I soon came to realize that the trailhead, located just before the road begins its climb to Stevens Pass, intimidates many hikers. Although you can access some lakes with a bit less elevation gain, if you're willing to sweat a bit more, this short, sweet hike will reward you in the end.

The cool waters of Hope and Mig Lakes are a great way to cool off on a hot summer day.

This trail gets your heart pumping from the beginning with a steep, dusty climb through an old clear-cut before entering the cool shade of the forest. Douglas-fir, hemlock, and a few old cedars keep you company as you steadily make your way up the valley. In 0.25 mile, the trail crosses a small footbridge in a large patch of huckleberry bushes. If you're here in late July or August, make sure to leave time to collect a midmorning snack or an afternoon treat.

Once you have had your fair share of berry goodness, continue your ascent through the woods. At 0.5 mile, a 15- to 20-foot cliff band intersects the trail. A short but precarious path branches off from here, providing a view into a mini-gorge through which Tunnel Creek bubbles; however, the view from the main trail is just as impressive.

From here, the trail wraps around the back side of the rock formation, keeping Tunnel Creek out of sight for another 0.5 mile. In 0.25 mile, the trail cuts through a swath of alders interspersed with devil's club, a tall, thorny plant that can bring the most hardcore of hikers to tears if they stumble into it. Soon you reenter the forest and cross a couple of small, steep creeks that are usually dry by mid- to late summer. Even without water, these drainages are impressive. Large, downed trees are strewn throughout the creekbed, crisscrossed like matchsticks, evidence of the large, wet avalanches that can rip through the area in the winter and early spring months.

An old slide path at the 1-mile mark provides another glimpse of Tunnel Creek. From here, it's a short climb back through the forest to the Alpine Lakes Wilderness boundary and the opaque waters of Hope Lake. A couple of smaller ponds are visible through the trees from a bench above the lake to the south. The large campsites around the lake will most likely be taken on the weekends. There's a vault toilet on the west side of the lake.

If you want to take a dip but feel the murky waters of Hope Lake are uninviting, head north to the clearer waters of Mig Lake. It's a quick trip, with a climb of just more than 300 feet in 0.5 mile. The trail wanders through a forest of fir and hemlock before topping out in a large meadow.

The trail slowly contours to the east through the parkland as it makes its way around the north side of the lake. As you approach the shoreline, keep an eye out for a well-used spur trail that branches right. The trail passes a

Hope and Mig Lakes

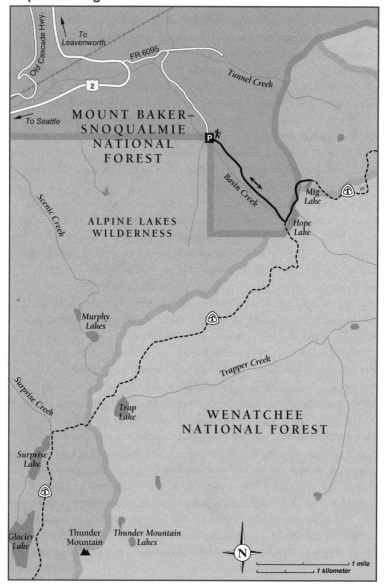

lily pad–filled pond before arriving at an overlook that also works well for picnics. The Pacific Crest Trail (PCT) continues around the north side of the lake, crossing a quaint stream that snakes through grasslands and marshy fields. A couple of good campsites are located on the northeast side of the lake (same side as the vault toilet). If you plan to camp at Hope or Mig Lake, be aware that campfires are prohibited within 0.5 mile of the lakes.

If you want to spend an entire day in this area, you have a couple options, depending on how much time and energy you have. Two miles north of Mig Lake is Swimming Deer Lake, and north of that lie the large, forested shores of Josephine Lake. If you can arrange transportation, you can continue north on the PCT, past Lake Susan Jane to Stevens Pass (7.5 miles from Mig Lake).

Heading south on the PCT from Hope Lake, the trail travels almost 4 miles along a ridge with great views to sparkling Trap Lake. If you're fortunate enough to have an extra vehicle, you can arrange another thru-hike: from Trap Lake, descend southwest to Trail 1060A and switchback steeply to the long, narrow Surprise Lake. Continue north on Trail 1060, a hiker-only route through the lush drainage of Surprise Creek (see Hike 19, page 129).

PERMIT INFORMATION Northwest Forest Pass ($30/year) required; see tinyurl.com/northwestforestpass for more information. Self-issued permits available at the trailhead.

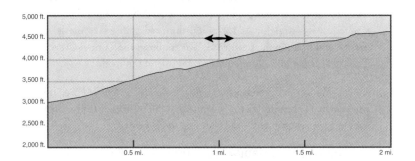

The forested shoreline of Mig Lake

DIRECTIONS From US 2 in Everett just east of I-5, drive east about 50 miles toward Stevens Pass. Continue 12 miles past the quiet town of Skykomish, cross the Tunnel Creek Bridge, and, just beyond the hairpin, turn right onto Forest Road 6095. At 0.8 mile, you'll reach a junction—go straight. At 1.2 miles, the road splits; take the left branch and head up the steep road. The trailhead for Tunnel Creek Trail 1061 is 0.1 mile along, on the right side of the road.

NOTE: *This trailhead is accessible only from the eastbound lane of US 2.* If you're driving west on US 2, continue past the trailhead, find a safe spot to turn around, and head back east to FR 6095.

GPS TRAILHEAD COORDINATES N47° 42.689' W121° 6.676'

21 | Chain and Doelle Lakes

> SCENERY: ☆ ☆ ☆ ☆   TRAIL CONDITION: ☆ ☆ ☆
>
> CHILDREN: ☆   DIFFICULTY: ☆ ☆ ☆ ☆
>
> SOLITUDE: ☆ ☆ ☆   DISTANCE: 22 miles
>
> HIKING TIME: 3–4 days
>
> GREEN TRAILS MAPS: *Stevens Pass 176 and Chiwaukum Mountains 177*
>
> OUTSTANDING FEATURES: Parkland meadows, views into some of the most remote areas in the Central Cascades, a multitude of alpine lakes—and solitude at the most stunning of these

A GOOD FRIEND AND FORMER U.S. Forest Service employee described this trip as including one of the best alpine lakes in the Central Cascades. And even though I scouted them in a torrential downpour, I agree with him: the lakes are amazing, and the solitude is worth every switchback. To get the most out of your trip, give yourself time to explore the high country that surrounds this truly magical place.

Your first 4 miles of hiking are going to be a far cry from a wilderness experience; busy trails, buzzing power lines, screaming chainsaws, and multiple ski lifts are just a few of the distractions you're likely to encounter. You are traveling through a ski area, after all.

That said, plenty of nature's distractions—such as fat, juicy huckleberries, the high-pitched whistle of a marmot as it waddles away to hide, and morning dewdrops in the leaf of a lupine—make this stretch enjoyable. Besides, the remaining 7 miles to the lakes more than makes up for the fact that the first few are less than ideal. Take this section for what it is and know that the best is yet to come.

The Pacific Crest Trail (PCT) begins with a short but steep hike into a nice stand of timber. You gradually reach open slopes and catch sight of the first-cut ski run at Stevens Pass. The original ski area, which differed drastically from what you see today, was developed back in 1937 by two avid skiers named Don Adams and Bruce Kehr. The two men obtained a permit from the U.S. Forest

Chain and Doelle Lakes

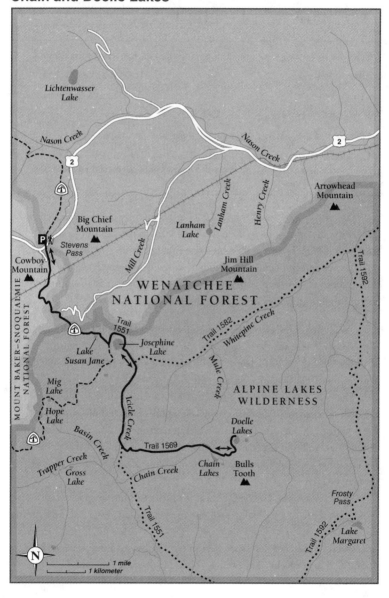

Lichtenwasser
Lake

Nason Creek

Nason Creek

2

2

Arrowhead
Mountain

Big Chief
Mountain

Lanham
Lake

Lanham Creek

Henry Creek

Mill Creek

Jim Hill
Mountain

P

Stevens
Pass

Cowboy
Mountain

WENATCHEE
NATIONAL FOREST

Trail
1551

Josephine
Lake

Trail 1582

Whitepine Creek

Trail 1592

Lake
Susan Jane

Mule Creek

Mig
Lake

ALPINE LAKES
WILDERNESS

MOUNT BAKER–SNOQUALMIE NATIONAL FOREST

Hope
Lake

Icicle Creek

Basin Creek

Trail 1569

Doelle
Lakes

Trapper Creek

Gross
Lake

Chain Creek

Chain
Lakes

Bulls
Tooth

Frosty
Pass

Trail 1551

Trail 1592

Lake
Margaret

N

1 mile

1 kilometer

Service, cut a small swath, bought supplies to build a $600 rope tow, and opened for business, charging skiers 5¢ for each ride up the tow.

At the time, you had two choices: make a 6-mile hike on the highway from the small town of Scenic, or purchase a one-way ticket on the *Great Northern Passenger* train, then hop an old school bus to the ski area. Eventually four rope tows were installed, but they were replaced in 1964 by the two-person chair you see today. The trail crosses under the chair, leaving the meadow and a bit of Stevens Pass history behind.

The trees for the next mile or so create a sight and sound barrier from the highway below and also provide shade, a welcome relief on a hot, buggy day. In 1.5 miles, you cross under the Tye Mill chair and begin a steady series of switchbacks. The trail ascends in the shadow of Cowboy Ridge, a recreational hot spot for backcountry skiers and snowboarders looking to test their skills in its steep, rocky terrain.

After a somewhat grinding climb, you eventually reach the ridgetop (5,120'), just east of the back side chairlift that descends into Mill Valley. Immediate views from this location aren't that impressive; however, once you get beyond the power lines and chairlifts, the views of what lies ahead should excite you. From here you can also see your route etched in a hillside far below.

To get there, descend a couple of rocky switchbacks and continue southeastward, as the trail travels below a long ridgeline known as Rooster Comb. As you make your way to the wilderness boundary, you encounter a few more artificial obstacles. At 3.3 miles, the trail cuts under the chairlift, goes through

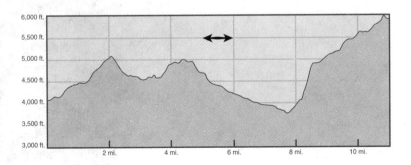

a boulder field, and pops out on a service road. Follow the signs across the road and resume your hike, heading under large, crackling power lines.

A short way from here is the Alpine Lakes Wilderness boundary. From this point, it's less than 1 mile to your first alpine lake, Susan Jane. The trail arrives at the south shore, which has good camping—a decent option if you have kids or time constraints. The area can be busy on weekends, so be prepared to share it.

From the lake, the PCT ascends a couple of switchbacks then rises past the east bank of Susan Jane as it climbs to a narrow pass. Pass a couple of unnamed ponds and, a little more than 1 mile from the lake, reach the junction with Icicle Creek Trail 1551. Turn north and head up to a small, grassy bench dotted with pools.

The trail descends steeply from here to the emerald green waters of Josephine Lake and the perfect spot to enjoy a leisurely lunch if you're just out for the day. This is also a popular place for backpackers looking for a quick escape from the hustle and bustle of the city. The shoreline was once almost loved to death, so respect areas that are being restored and camp only in designated sites.

If you're continuing to Chain Lakes, cross the outlet stream, which is the headwaters of Icicle Creek, and descend a couple switchbacks. From here, the trail begins a 2-mile brushy descent down the Icicle Creek drainage. In 0.6 mile, the trail reaches the junction with White Pine Trail 1582. Continue following Icicle Creek down the valley, and in 1.5 miles, the trail crosses the creek on logs and rocks. Just beyond the crossing, there's a nice little camp that would break up the hike, but avoid the crowds at Josephine Lake.

A quarter mile past the campsite is the turnoff for Chain Lakes Trail 1569. Head east up this trail and get ready to do some serious climbing. Steep, tight, rugged switchbacks characterize the start of this 2,000-foot climb to the lake, after which you encounter a seemingly never-ending uphill hike, on which the phrase "Am I there yet?" may run through your head.

In 2.5 miles (5,628'), you're finally there, and trust me when I say it's worth the effort. The trail arrives at the first of the three lakes and runs along its

OPPOSITE: *Lakeside camping at Chain Lakes*

long, narrow southern shoreline. The valley broadens as you approach the second lake, and the true magic of this place is revealed. The lakes rest in a horseshoe basin of craggy ridgelines whose lower slopes are littered with fields of white granite boulders. Parkland meadows brim with flowers and tiny creeks trickle from the snowy slopes. You'll find great camping here, but remember, this area is fragile: camp only at designated sites or in areas that have already been used.

Once you're settled in, consider an after-dinner hike to Doelle Lakes. To get there, cross the stream between the first and second lakes, and, when the trail forks, take the left branch. The trail rises quickly through talus and offers great views back toward all three lakes. In a little less than 1 mile, the trail reaches a small stand of trees, makes a couple of switchbacks, and rises through a notch in Bulls Tooth Ridge.

A bird's-eye view of Upper Doelle Lake

Views to the northeast allow you to see just how different the east side of the crest can be. The landscape changes drastically from lush, thick forests to open, much drier slopes. Motivated hikers can descend a few hundred feet through heather to the north shore of the upper lake. Those who feel they have hiked enough can simply retrace their steps to camp and head home.

Hikers looking for a true adventure can make a loop—but only if you have experience with cross-country travel and route finding. Continue east from Lower Doelle Lake to Trail 1570, which is no longer maintained. This often hard-to-find trail travels east then southeast to Frosty Pass. From there, you can take Wildhorse Creek Trail 1592 north to Whitepine Creek Trail 1582. Follow this desolate trail back to Icicle Creek and retrace your route north to Stevens Pass.

PERMIT INFORMATION Northwest Forest Pass ($30/year) required; see tinyurl.com/northwestforestpass for more information. Self-issued permits available at the trailhead.

DIRECTIONS Drive US 2 to the summit of Stevens Pass (about 64 miles east of Seattle). Turn right (south) and follow the signs for the southbound PCT trailhead, in the far eastern lot (Parking Lot E).

GPS TRAILHEAD COORDINATES N47° 44.799' W121° 5.292'

North: Stevens Pass to Canadian Border

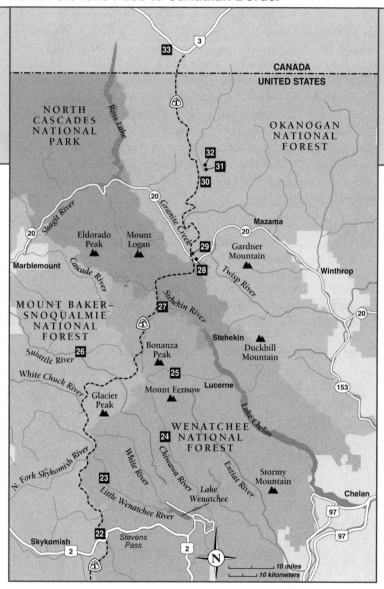

PART 3: NORTH

Stevens Pass to Canadian Border

Azurite Peak makes a dramatic backdrop for the PCT (see Hike 30, page 197).

22 Lake Valhalla

SCENERY: ✿ ✿ ✿ ✿	TRAIL CONDITION: ✿ ✿ ✿ ✿
CHILDREN: ✿ ✿ ✿ ✿	DIFFICULTY: ✿ ✿ ✿
SOLITUDE: ✿ ✿	HIKING TIME: 4 hours

DISTANCE: 8.5 miles (5.5 miles to lake)

GREEN TRAILS MAP: *Benchmark Mountain 144*

OUTSTANDING FEATURES: Alpine lake with good fishing, easy access for an overnight hike with children, and great meadows

THIS ROUTE'S VERSATILITY MAKES IT a great option if weather, time, or hiking partners change. A car shuttle is required for the approach I describe; however, you can hike out-and-back from the Stevens Pass or Smithbrook trailheads.

🚶 From the rugged terrain of Stevens Pass, the trail starts on an old, slightly inclining maintenance road that parallels the highway for about the first 1.5 miles. Stunning views to the east, diverse wildflowers, and occasional glimpses into the quaint neighborhood of Yodelin should distract you from the highway noise.

After a couple miles, the trail begins to wrap around the north-facing slopes of Skyline Ridge as it heads west up the Nason Creek drainage. At this point, you cross over the abandoned east entrance of the Cascade Tunnel, part of the Great Northern Railroad (GNR). By far the most rugged section of the GNR, a series of tunnels was built in the Stevens Pass corridor between 1897 and 1929 to protect the trains from the constant avalanches cascading from the slopes above. The worst avalanche fatality in the United States occurred at the west entrance of the tunnel, where 96 people on their way from Leavenworth to Seattle were buried in a slide while waiting for weather conditions to improve. Clear-cutting and forest fires started by steam locomotive sparks were a major cause of the slope's instability.

From here, the trail begins a slightly steeper ascent. Your first rewarding view of Lichtenberg Mountain is at 2.3 miles as you enter an open boulder field.

Just before you hit the 3-mile mark, you'll see a large, flat rock off on the right side of the trail, the perfect perch for a water break. The rock is conveniently located just before a series of switchbacks that leads to the headwaters of Nason Creek. As you enter the basin, take the spur trail to a small campsite tucked in a stand of alpine fir atop a knoll. This is a great spot to pitch a tent if you're looking for a short excursion away from the crowds. Since the mosquitoes are thick in this area, an outing in late August or September might be your best bet.

From the meadow, the trail begins a steady climb as it gains the last 1,500 feet to the lake. A flat bench at the 4-mile mark creates a bit of a "false summit" as the gradient levels out and you can't help but imagine the lake is "just around the corner." The view here is still spectacular, with fields of buttercups dotting the landscape. The trail climbs a forested slope for another mile before rounding a ridge and traversing a large boulder field with great views to the south and east. From here, it's a short distance to your first glimpse of Lake Valhalla's crystal-clear waters in the shadow of Lichtenberg's imposing west face.

The trail descends to another meadow that's tempting to camp in; note, however, that restoration efforts are under way, and you must camp in designated sites on the lakeshore. If you are planning to camp at the lake or are looking for a good place to stop for lunch, continue on the spur trail that descends southeast to reach the northwest shores of the lake. It's worth hiking down there to see the schools of trout swimming up and around the lake's inlet. This is a popular place with day hikers, dog walkers, anglers, and backpackers on weekends, so be prepared to share this beautiful location.

If you plan to continue to the Smithbrook Trailhead, hike back to the junction and head east on the Pacific Crest Trail (PCT). Along the way, you'll get a breathtaking view of the lake with the snowcapped mountains of the #3 Chiwakum range in the background. Even if you're not doing this as a thru-hike, it's well worth the effort to hike up to this vantage point.

Approximately 0.5 mile from the junction, you reach a saddle where snow can linger until late July. Use caution when descending from the saddle even if it's sunny and warm. As the trail descends to the northeast, Lichtenberg changes form once again as steep creeks pour over large granite slabs to make their way into the gurgling waters of Smith Brook.

Lake Valhalla

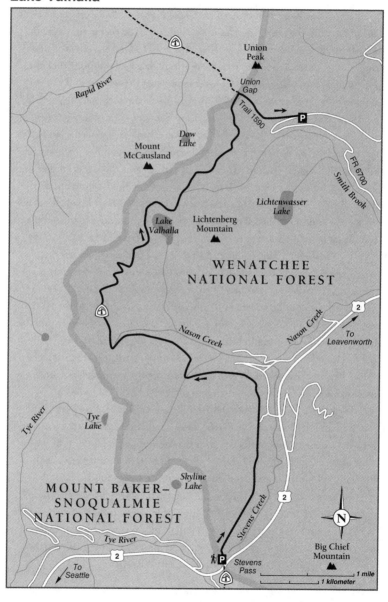

It's now obvious where the majority of hikers came from, as it's just 3 miles to the lake from the Smithbrook Trailhead. However, the climb is much steeper, gaining 800 feet in the first 0.8 mile. At 2.2 miles, you reach a junction. The PCT continues north toward Union Gap, while the Smithbrook Trail makes its steep descent to Forest Road 6700. If your feet need a pick-me-up, take a minute to soak them in Smith Brook's healing waters.

PERMIT INFORMATION Northwest Forest Pass ($30/year) required; see tinyurl.com/northwestforestpass for more information. Self-issued permits available at the trailhead.

DIRECTIONS

TO STEVENS PASS TRAILHEAD: Drive US 2 to the summit of Stevens Pass (about 64 miles east of Seattle), and turn left into Parking Lot D, opposite the main entrance to the ski area, on the north side of the highway. The trailhead is behind the electric-power substation in the far right corner of the parking lot.

TO SMITHBROOK TRAILHEAD: From Stevens Pass, continue east on US 2 and turn left onto Forest Road 6700 in 4 miles. Follow the gravel road 3.1 miles to the Smithbrook Trailhead, on the left side of the road.

GPS TRAILHEAD COORDINATES N47° 44.799' W121° 5.292'

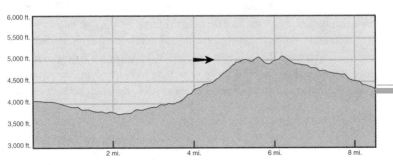

23 Cady Ridge to Kodak Peak

SCENERY: ✿ ✿ ✿ ✿ ✿	TRAIL CONDITION: ✿ ✿ ✿
CHILDREN: ✿	DIFFICULTY: ✿ ✿ ✿ ✿
SOLITUDE: ✿ ✿ ✿	DISTANCE: 18 miles
HIKING TIME: 2–3 days	GREEN TRAILS MAP: *Benchmark Mountain 144*

OUTSTANDING FEATURES: Alpine ridge walks with sweeping views into Glacier Peak Wilderness, a variety of backpacking loops, great wildflowers, and abundant wildlife

IF YOU FIND YOURSELF with a bundle of vacation days, I strongly suggest taking them all at once, grab your pack, and head out to this breathtaking area's myriad trails. If you arrive to discover a packed parking lot, don't worry. The endless routes within the first 0.5 mile send people off in all directions.

Give yourself a few days to explore this amazing area. Plenty of trail systems allow you to access cool routes that can be hiked as extended backpacking loops or as out-and-back day hikes from camp. The route described here ascends Cady Ridge to the Pacific Crest Trail (PCT) and heads north to Kodak Peak, where numerous hiking options are available once you ascend a bit. The many other trails referenced along the way will help you plan an unforgettable trip.

From the lower parking lot, take Cady Creek Trail 1501. The path dips down to the crystal-clear waters of the Little Wenatchee River and crosses it over a large, sturdy bridge. In 0.5 mile, you'll reach a junction with Cady Creek Trail 1501, which heads west up the brushy banks of Cady Creek to the PCT. Turn north onto Cady Ridge Trail 1532 and begin a series of long, mellow switchbacks through the cool shade of the forest for the next mile or so.

Enjoy this section because, just as the canopy seems to open, the switchbacks get tighter and the tread gets rougher. Although only a mile, this steep, dusty section makes you feel that you're earning every bit of the reward that awaits. Just when you start to wonder if it's worth it, the gradient eases and the

OPPOSITE: *A sign marks the turnoff for Kodiak Peak.*

Cady Ridge to Kodak Peak

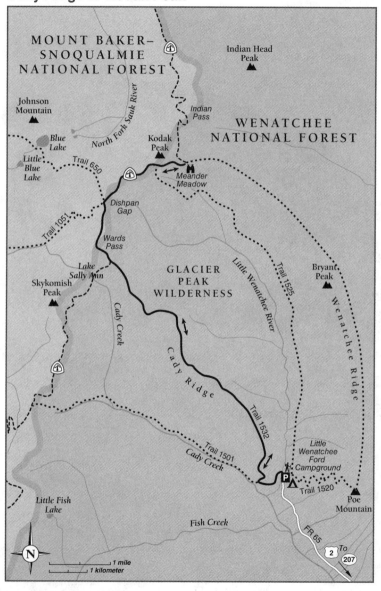

first of many vistas comes into view. The Wenatchee ridge rises across the valley to the east, its rocky ridgeline formed by the extensions from Long-fellow Mountain and Bryant Peak.

From here, the trail wanders in and out of forests and meadows, alter-nating from the east side to the west side of the ridge, with a few sections actually traveling along the ridge itself until it reaches a high point at 5,600 feet. If you were impressed with the views to here, you'll feel downright giddy as you descend from the high point onto the broad, open slopes of upper Cady Ridge. Views open in just about every direction as the trail makes a steady descent along the west side of the ridge. Grassy knolls between fields of low-lying huckleberry bushes provide the perfect perch for those wanting to take a load off to rest tired feet and sore legs.

Press on as the trail gradually descends, losing 200 feet in a little less than 1 mile. As it begins to flatten out, you'll pass a nice camp nestled in a patch of alpine firs with a great view of Glacier Peak and Meander Meadow. This is a good choice if you want to avoid the crowds that tend to gather on and around the PCT. There's no water source here, but Lake Sally Ann is a little more than 0.5 mile away—you'll want to check it out anyway.

From the camp, the trail makes a steep, short climb to the PCT (note that Cady Ridge Trail is not signed here). You have a couple of options from this point. Heading south along the PCT, in 0.5 mile you arrive at Lake Sally Ann, its calm, greenish-blue waters contrasting sharply with the grey and black hues of the rocky crags that rise steeply above. This spot is a must-see, and a dip in the chilly water is a must-do after the steep, dusty climb it took

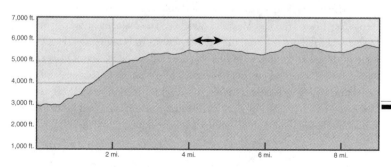

to get here. The lake has ample camping, but fires are prohibited. You can make a loop hike from here by continuing south to Cady Pass and heading out Cady Creek Trail 1501, for a round-trip hike of about 16 miles.

To continue to Kodak Peak from the junction, head north along the PCT. The trail soon crosses a small stream before winding its way up switchbacks to bring you to Wards Pass. Once again, you'll be awe inspired, as you look west at Monte Cristo, a monstrous mound of jagged rock and snowbound slopes.

From the pass, hike around the west side of Point 5905. As you approach a small saddle on the north side of the point, you get a great view of Kodak Peak's knobby summit. In another mile, you reach Dishpan Gap, a four-way junction affording even more opportunities to check out this magical area. If you want to explore some of the drainages, head down the Skykomish River on Trail 1051, up Pass Creek on Trail 1053 to Cady Pass, and out Cady Creek back to the Little Wenatchee Ford Campground. This loop's total distance is about 23 miles.

You can also make a quick trip to the rockbound waters of Blue Lake northwest of Dishpan Gap. Diehard loop hikers can continue south from the lake to Little Blue Lake and hike back to Dishpan Gap on Trail 650, adding a little more than 5 miles to the hike. For those continuing along the PCT, drop northeast around a bowl containing a couple of feeder streams that eventually join the Little Wenatchee. As the trail begins to head east, two rock pyramids seem to jut up out of nowhere. Side by side, these two unnamed features provide a striking contrast to the broad ridgelines and lush meadows that dominate most of this area.

These two rock formations become visible as you approach Little Wenatchee River Trail and Meander Meadow. The majority of overnighters in this area head out this trail for a pleasant one- or two-night backpacking trip. If you're feeling more adventurous, follow the PCT as it makes its way around Kodak Peak, through meadows of cotton grass, heather, and hellebore. In a little less than 1 mile, you reach a junction; a climbers' trail heads west to the very top of Kodak Peak, an unmaintained trail heads east to Wenatchee Ridge, and the PCT continues its steady push north.

If you're looking for solitude and adventure, there's a great cross-country hike that follows the Wenatchee Ridge—no trails, no people, and no water by midsummer combine to create an unforgettable experience. This route is recommended only for experienced backpackers prepared to do some serious traversing and ridgeline route finding over rugged terrain rarely traveled by anyone other than hunters enjoying the high hunt in the fall. The ridge eventually joins Poe Mountain Trail 1520, which descends steeply, losing 3,000 feet in 2.5 miles on its way down to Little Wenatchee Trail. When you reach this junction, turn south to reach the parking lot in about 0.25 mile.

PERMIT INFORMATION Northwest Forest Pass ($30/year) required; see tinyurl.com/northwestforestpass for more information. Self-issued permits available at the trailhead.

DIRECTIONS From Stevens Pass, drive east for 19 miles on US 2, and turn left (north) onto WA 207 toward Lake Wenatchee. In 4.2 miles, the road crosses the Wenatchee River—take the left fork just after the bridge. Continue on this road 6 more miles until it reaches another fork, and then take the left branch across some open fields and over the White River. Follow this road, which eventually turns into FR 6500, for about 15 miles, until it ends at Little Wenatchee Ford Campground.

GPS TRAILHEAD COORDINATES N47° 55.039' W121° 5.251'

24 Little Giant Pass

SCENERY: ✿ ✿ ✿ ✿ ✿	TRAIL CONDITION: ✿ ✿
CHILDREN: ✿	DIFFICULTY: ✿ ✿ ✿ ✿
SOLITUDE: ✿ ✿ ✿ ✿	DISTANCE: 10 miles
HIKING TIME: 6–8 hours	GREEN TRAILS MAP: *Holden 113*

OUTSTANDING FEATURES: A magnificent view into the enchanting Napeequa Valley, a chilly river crossing to get the adrenalin pumping, and a somewhat grueling climb that earns you a hearty dinner at the end of the day

THIS HIKE USED TO BE part of a temporary Pacific Crest Trail (PCT) reroute created in 2003 after severe flooding in the Glacier Peak Wilderness rendered nearly 50 miles of trail inaccessible for more than a decade. Many hikers chose to bypass this part of the detour due to its steep, rugged terrain and an unavoidable river crossing. Although Little Giant Pass is no longer part of the PCT since the washed-out section reopened in 2011, it remains one of my favorite hikes. It's best to do this hike at the end of season, when water levels are low and you feel strong after conditioning yourself all summer.

Worth every ounce of effort: the majestic Napeequa Valley

👣   Pulling up to the trailhead, you may wonder where all the other cars are. Well, for starters, the hike begins with a nerve-racking crossing of the Chiwawa River, which early in the season can turn back even the most adventurous of spirits. Secondly, it's a lung burner on the way up and a knee pounder on the way down, gaining 4,000 feet in a little more than 4.5 miles. Lastly, on a warm summer day, sections of the trail can cook, and on a rainy day, it turns into a muddy, rutted-out mess.

So why would you even consider tackling this hike? Well, there are numerous reasons, but solitude, incredible views that will literally take your breath away, and bright-green grassy meadows splashed with a colorful assortment of wildflowers are my favorites.

To begin, follow the trail west a short way to the Chiwawa River ford (2,600'). By late in the season, it's possible to wade across this frigid river; in any case, be prepared to get wet. If the river looks high, it may be worth spending a little extra time in search of a logjam to scamper across. If neither wading nor scampering is feasible, save this hike for another day. Fortunately, a number of wonderful hikes lie farther down the road.

Once you safely cross the river, the trail can be tricky to find. Locate the most well-traveled path, and follow it along the overgrown roads that were once a part of Maple Creek Campground. In 0.25 mile, the trail crosses Maple Creek on another somewhat confusing maze of trails. Pick up the main trail on the north side of the creek, and follow it as it parallels the creek a short way.

Enjoy leisurely switchbacks that wind back and forth through stands of pine trees for the next mile or so. After this, you face a steep, grueling climb to a saddle. While catching your breath, take a look around at the stands of dying trees, a sign of the elusive pine bark beetle that has affected hundreds of thousands of acres in the Cascade Range.

Bark beetles are a part of the natural environment, and in a healthy forest they contribute by creating habitats for other animals and assist in fire ecology, a vital component for pine forests in particular. Forests affected by years of drought, poor management practices, and fire suppression are much more susceptible to massive outbreaks of beetles, which burrow into the bark, gradually killing the trees from within. Many land management agencies are

Little Giant Pass

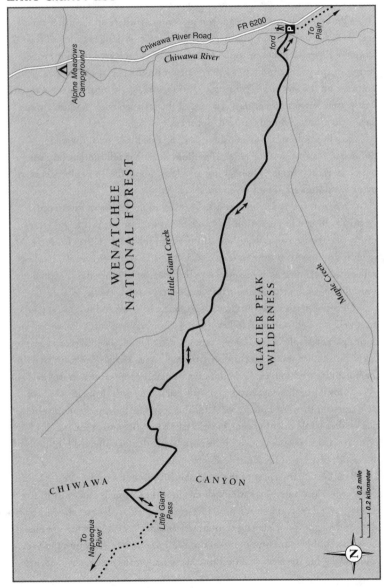

studying this epidemic in an effort to mitigate large-scale occurrences and reduce the risk of catastrophic fires that can rip through these patches of standing dead timber.

Leaving the saddle, the trail descends to a crossing of the South Fork of Little Giant Creek (4,000'). The few campsites on either side of the creek have a tendency to be buggy during the summer months.

After crossing the creek, avoid a trail that branches north through a grassy meadow. Follow the trail that turns upstream, paralleling the creek.

Take a breath because now it's time to climb. From here, the trail gains 2,400 feet in 2.5 miles. On the bright side, views continually open as you climb ever higher into the alpine. A quarter mile from the creek crossing, you enter a stand of burnt timber, remnants from the Maple Creek fire that burned 2,300 acres back in the summer of 2003.

Continue to climb as the trail becomes steep, narrow, and extremely rutted in places. This stretch evidences nothing like the caliber of trail maintenance many PCT thru-hikers come to expect, which is why some of the less hardy ones avoid this section altogether.

Around 3 miles the trail cuts through a broad ridge composed of schist, and views into Little Giant Creek to the north and Maple Creek to the south offer a welcome distraction from the pain in your legs. The trail is a bit brushy in places, but in another mile, it transitions into lush meadows carpeted with wildflowers. A long traverse eventually brings you to a notch in the middle of Chiwawa Ridge known as Little Giant Pass (6,400').

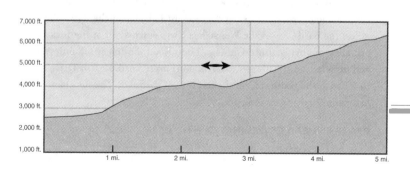

The views from here will literally take your breath away. The milky blue water of the Napeequa River snakes its way through the valley far below, and cascading waterfalls tumble from all sides through a patchwork of greenery. Clark Mountain's shimmering slopes are the most prominent feature to the west and, on a clear day, Glacier Peak is visible just beyond the head of the valley. For even more stunning views, take a walk up either of two knolls, one north and one south of the pass.

If the views from here just aren't enough, an unmaintained trail drops steeply from the pass down to the valley floor (4,400'). A warning before you go scurrying off: the trail resembles more of a sheep trail than a hiking trail and is barely visible at times. This route is suitable only for experienced hikers—and, remember, what goes down, must come up. You can camp on gravel bars along the river if you need to.

If you've had enough for one day, simply reverse your route. You'll quickly learn why so many PCT hikers cursed this section. (At least the time goes by fast.) Soon you'll be back at the Chiwawa River crossing. Unlike the first time through, the second time feels so good to your tired legs that you can almost hear them say "Ahhhh" when they hit the ice-cold water. Enjoy the moment before heading to the far bank and returning to your car.

PERMIT INFORMATION Northwest Forest Pass ($30/year) required; see tinyurl.com/northwestforestpass for more information. Self-issued permits available at the trailhead.

DIRECTIONS From Stevens Pass, drive east for 19 miles on US 2, and turn left (north) onto WA 207 toward Lake Wenatchee. In 4.2 miles, the road crosses the Wenatchee River—turn right at the fork just after the bridge onto Chiwawa Loop Road. Follow it 1.4 miles and turn left onto Chiwawa River Road (Forest Road 6200). Drive 19 miles to the trailhead, on the left side of the road. The shoulder has room for a few cars to park.

GPS TRAILHEAD COORDINATES N48° 1.538' W120° 49.690'

25 Suiattle River to Miners Ridge,
Including Image Lake

SCENERY: ✿ ✿ ✿ ✿ ✿   TRAIL CONDITION: ✿ ✿ ✿ ✿

CHILDREN: ✿   DIFFICULTY: ✿ ✿ ✿ ✿

SOLITUDE: ✿ ✿ ✿   DISTANCE: 33 miles

HIKING TIME: 3 days   GREEN TRAILS MAPS: *Glacier Peak 112, Holden 115*

OUTSTANDING FEATURES: One of the most picturesque (and most photographed) backcountry lakes in Washington State, spectacular 360-degree vistas from a volunteer-staffed lookout, and stunning views of Glacier Peak and the rugged North Cascades.

AFTER NEARLY A DECADE OF BEING closed due to massive flooding in 2003 and 2006, Suiattle River Road reopened in 2015, and it was like unlocking a buried treasure chest. Many of the roads and trails in the Glacier Peak area are still washed out, with no prospect of ever being fixed. The Suiattle River is now the primary access point for some of the most remote and breathtaking terrain this state has to offer.

🚶🚶 To begin this hike, head to the far end of the parking lot, where the road ends and the trail begins. As you leave the trailhead, you almost immediately come to the Sulphur Mountain Trail, a brutal route that climbs 4,200 feet in 5 miles. This trail sees minimal use due to its steep, rugged nature, so if you're looking for solitude the next time you head out, this is a great option. For this hike, continue along the Suiattle's mellow gradient, and quickly come to the Glacier Peak Wilderness boundary and the trailhead register.

In just under a mile, the trail arrives at an unsigned junction with Milk Creek Trail 790. The bridge spanning the Suiattle washed away during the floods, and the trail has since been abandoned (no immediate plans have been made to fix this trail).

From the junction, the trail travels through old-growth forests of Douglas-fir and western hemlock above the wild and scenic Suiattle River. Even at its lowest levels, the Suiattle displays its power in the high, eroded

Suiattle River to Miners Ridge, Including Image Lake

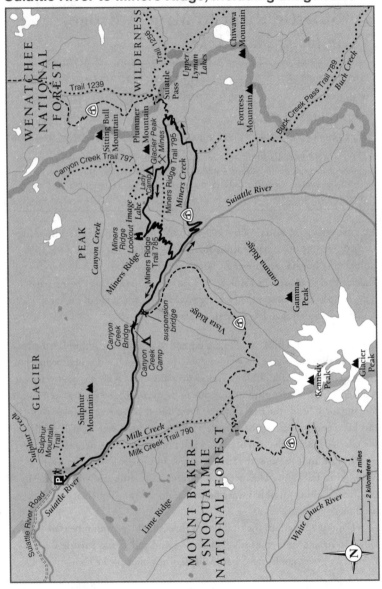

banks that surround it. The milky-grey water eventually meets up with the Sauk River, which then flows into the Skagit before dumping into the Puget Sound. The Suiattle and Sauk Rivers are protected under the National Wild and Scenic Rivers Act that was enacted under President Lyndon B. Johnson back in 1968. Views of this mighty river come and go as the trail climbs in and out of a series of steep creeks.

At 3 miles, the trail comes to its first camp. The camp has room for one or two tents, but water is limited late in the summer. A much more established camp lies around the 6.5-mile mark at Canyon Creek. This is a great, although popular, site with lots of options. As you approach the camp, a trail breaks off of the main trail to the right and takes you to an upper bench with two sites. These sites are a more secluded option if the main camp is occupied. Social trails leave from the sites down to the main camp, where there are four or five tent sites, a pit toilet, and access to Canyon Creek. If these options aren't available, look for a small camp with a pit toilet just after you cross the beautiful Canyon Creek Bridge.

In 0.3 mile after crossing Canyon Creek, the trail arrives at the Pacific Crest Trail (PCT). To continue this hike, you'll want to head north on the PCT. If time permits, it's definitely worth hiking the extra 5 minutes south on the PCT to the impressive suspension bridge that now spans across the Suiattle River. The original bridge was swept away by the massive floods of 2003 that washed away nearly every bridge within the Glacier Peak Wilderness. The Suiattle River Bridge project was completed in 2011 and included a 3.5-mile reroute from the original PCT.

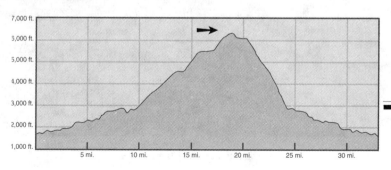

One of the most iconic lakes in the state lives up to its reputation.

Continuing on the northern PCT, the trail travels high above the river and in a little over 2 miles reaches an established camp. The camp itself is fairly unremarkable; however, there's plenty of space for a larger group, with three sites on the north side and one site and a pit toilet on the south side of the trail. This site is also located a short distance from the junction for Miners Ridge Trail 785. Many hikers simply do an out-and-back to Image Lake via this trail, but I am partial to loops. For this description, take note that this will be your descent route from Image Lake.

From the junction, continue southeast along the PCT as it does a gradual descent toward the Suiattle. The trail briefly travels along the sandy banks of the river with stunning views of Glacier Peak (10,541') before heading back into the forest. At 1.5 miles from the Miners Ridge Trail junction, the trail arrives at PCT Camp, a great little site with easy access to the river.

Leaving camp, the trail passes the old, abandoned PCT before ascending a series of long switchbacks, then turns east up Miners Creek. Views to the north toward Miners Ridge come and go as the trail works its way in and out of the steep creeks that pour down from Middle Ridge. At 4.5 miles from PCT Camp, the trail arrives at a junction with Buck Creek Pass Trail 789. Remnants of an old camp can be found here, but a sign states that it's no longer maintained.

Enjoyable, mostly level walking brings you to the crossing of Miners Creek. A site for one tent lies just off the trail, and a footbridge over the creek provides easy access to water. This is a great spot to take a break before beginning a 1,000-foot climb to the junction for Miners Ridge.

Leaving the creek, the PCT begins a climb to the northwest on its way toward Suiattle Pass. As you climb, views begin to expand with Chiwawa (8,459') and Fortress (8,760') Mountains dominating the landscape to the southeast and the mighty glaciated slopes of Glacier Peak coming into full view to the southwest.

In just under 2 miles from the Miners Creek crossing, you arrive at the signed junction for Miners Ridge Trail 795. Take this trail as it turns west, crosses a creek, and in a short distance arrives at the first in a series of abandoned Glacier Peak mines. A small shrine of old mining relics is the first

Taking in the views from the Miners Ridge Lookout

indication you have arrived. A collapsed cabin can be found tucked in the woods on the north side of the trail. A couple of small tent sites are located just off the main trail as you arrive, and another site can be found lying in a small stand of trees near the cabin. There is no pit toilet.

From the mine, the trail crosses a steep creek on a series of large, flat boulders. In just over a mile from camp, it passes through an impressive slide path, where a massive pile of trees can be seen far in the valley below. Shortly beyond the path, the remnants of a second cabin can be seen just north of the trail.

Just past the cabin site is the signed junction for Lady Camp and Image Lake. Miners Cabin Trail 795 continues west, traversing below Miners Ridge for 2 miles before meeting up with Miners Ridge Trail 785 (your descent route).

Head north up a long series of switchbacks, and in less than a mile, you arrive at Lady Camp (6,200'), the horse camp for the Image Lake–Miners Ridge area. I honestly wasn't sure what to expect when I finally made it up to the high country (you've hiked almost 20 miles by this point, through mostly forested terrain), but I was overwhelmed with just how spectacular it was. *The Sound of Music* was the first thing that popped into my head, although that image doesn't include the glistening white slopes of Glacier Peak in the background. Needless to say, you won't be disappointed with your first views of the flower-filled meadows that make up Miners Ridge.

The trail for Lady Camp is located in a stand of trees just to the right of the main trail. The name comes from a tree carving located within that camp of a native woman that dates back to the early 19th century. There's room for one or two tents and hitching posts. To access the pit toilet, head west on the main trail through the meadow, and look for a signed spur trail on the south side that heads toward a small stand of trees.

To continue to Image Lake, follow the trail 0.8 mile to a signed junction for the unmaintained Canyon Creek Trail 797. Continue toward Image Lake (6,050'), and in less than 0.5 mile, you'll have finally arrived. Signs are posted at just about every junction to let you know that hikers and horse packers have made a large impact on the area over the years. Please do your part and use only existing trails and camp at the designated site on the south side of the lake.

From the lake, plenty of options for further exploration are available. Hiking up Miners Ridge offers unbeatable views to the north toward Dome Peak (8,920'), Sitting Bull (7,760'), and North Cascades National Park. Plummer Mountain (7,870') lies east of Miners Ridge and is a popular climbing objective from Image Lake. If you're feeling adventurous, a brushy day hike along the Canyon Creek Trail can be made for those with solid route finding experience. A quick hike to the north side of the lake provides a great spot to photograph one of the most picturesque lakes in the state.

As you'll quickly realize, it's hard to tear yourself away from this place. When you do get ready to leave, be sure you have plenty of time to visit the Miners Ridge Lookout (6,120'). From the lake, continue west along the Miners Ridge Trail, and in just under a mile, you reach the 0.3-mile spur trail that takes you to the lookout. The lookout was built in 1953 and is the third one constructed on this site. The first lookout was a 10-foot by 10-foot cedar-shake cabin built around 1926. This lookout has a rich history surrounding it, and the tradition continues with the friendly U.S. Forest Service volunteers who staff it today.

To return to the Suiattle River Trail, prepare to do some knee pounding. The trail squiggles its way down a series of switchbacks, losing 3,200 feet in a little over 5 miles. From the lookout junction, it's 2.3 miles to the intersection with Miners Cabin Trail, where you'll find a forested camp with a pit toilet. Continue descending the Miners Ridge Trail, and in approximately 3 miles, you'll arrive back at the PCT. Head south to the Suiattle River Trail, and in 9.5 miles arrive back at the trailhead parking lot.

PERMIT INFORMATION Northwest Forest Pass ($30/year) required; see tinyurl.com/northwestforestpass for more information. Self-issued permits available at the trailhead.

DIRECTIONS From Darrington, drive north for about 8 miles on WA 530 to the signed turnoff for Suiattle River Road (Forest Road 26). Turn right (east) and follow the road 24.5 miles to its end. The road is paved for the first 10 miles and is gravel for the last 14.5.

GPS TRAILHEAD COORDINATES N48° 8.719' W121° 6.790'

26 Lyman Lakes and Suiattle Pass

SCENERY: ✿ ✿ ✿ ✿	TRAIL CONDITION: ✿ ✿ ✿
CHILDREN: ✿ ✿ ✿	DIFFICULTY: ✿ ✿ ✿
SOLITUDE: ✿ ✿ ✿	HIKING TIME: 2–5 days

DISTANCE: 22 miles out-and-back to the PCT, 38 miles to Stehekin Road

GREEN TRAILS MAP: *Holden 113*

OUTSTANDING FEATURES: Cascading waterfalls, turquoise-blue lakes, glaciers, and colorful alpine meadows

THIS TRAIL BARELY INTERSECTS THE Pacific Crest Trail (PCT), but it was too good to leave out. You could continue out Agnes Creek along the PCT. If you don't have time to do it as a thru-hike, an overnight to the Lyman Lakes is just as spectacular, and there's plenty to explore from camp. If you're looking for a shorter hike or you have children with you, Hart Lake, only 4 miles from Holden Village, is a great, though popular, option.

🚶🚶 The trail begins from the remote Lutheran village of Holden. Exploration of this area began back in 1877, when railroad companies sent surveyors to find a route through the Central Cascades. Obviously, they didn't find one, but their journey led to an influx of prospectors in search of mining claims.

In 1896, after years of roaming the hills and valleys around Lake Chelan, James Henry Holden staked his first claim. Unfortunately, Holden would not live to see a working mine, as it would be another 42 years and nearly $3 million worth of investments before the first shipment of copper, gold, and zinc concentrate would make it into production. The mine prospered from 1938 to 1957, producing $100 million in metals. After World War II, the price of metal dropped; nearly all of the resources had been extracted, forcing the mine to shut down in 1957.

The Howe Sound Company bought the business in 1928, salvaging most of the mining equipment. It tried to sell the village for $100,000. In the end, a persistent buyer from the Lutheran Bible Institute (known today as Trinity

Lyman Lakes and Suiattle Pass

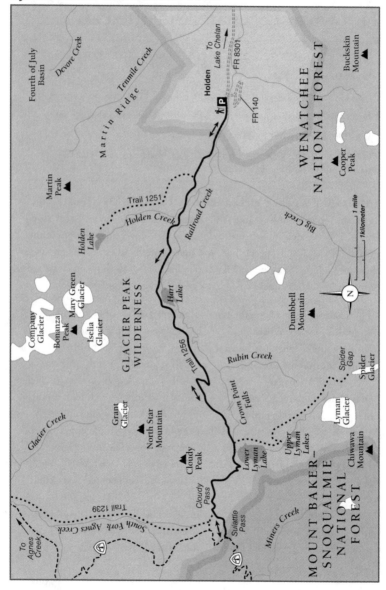

Lutheran College), named Wes Prieb, bought it for $1. Prieb raised money and brought in volunteers to restore the buildings and eventually turn it into what you see today. The village is open to everyone, so, if time permits, make a reservation to stay a night or two and explore a bit of Washington history.

To get to the trailhead from the village, head west 0.75 mile through town on the main (and only) dirt road, past remnants of the old mining town. From the trailhead, the trail skirts a washed-out section of road and then resumes its course on the dirt road. A 0.25-mile hike brings you to Glacier Peak Wilderness, where the road turns into a well-maintained, heavily used trail.

In a little less than a mile from the trailhead, you reach the turnoff for Holden Lake. This is a popular, yet strenuous day hike for anglers and visitors staying at Holden. Beyond the junction, the trail travels along a broad valley bottom with stands of pine, aspen, and cottonwood. Views of North Star open to the west, Dumbbell Mountain rises sharply from the Big Creek drainage to the southwest, and Copper Mountain can be seen to the south.

Cross the outlet of Holden Lake on a footbridge around the 2-mile mark; the trail enters the forest for 0.5 mile. You have open views again as you reach a field filled with grasses, sedges, shrubs, and snags. Railroad Creek moves ever so slowly, parallel to the trail.

This mellow, flat section soon ends, and the gradient steepens as you climb the last 300 feet to Hart Lake (3,956'). The trail tops out 100 feet or so above the shoreline and then descends on the north side of the lake. Tucked among crackling aspens and rustling cottonwoods on the west shoreline, near the lake's

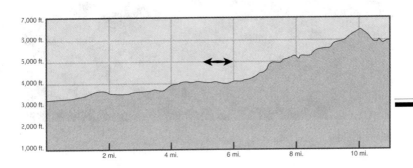

Hiking near the Lyman Lakes

inlet, are some great campsites. A night here is a nice way to break up the hike if you decide to head out on the same day you catch the shuttle to Holden.

The trail continues up Railroad Creek, crossing it not long after leaving Hart Lake. Waterfalls dominate the scenery for the next mile. Crown Point Falls rumbles loudly up the drainage, and unnamed falls and steep creeks tumble from the lower flanks of mighty Bonanza Peak (9,511'), the highest nonglaciated peak in Washington.

Rebel Camp is 4.8 miles from the trailhead. This site is forested, but views are fairly open and a small creek flows nearby. If you lack time or energy, this is another good place to stop before the dusty, brushy, 1,500-foot climb. You're rewarded with close-up views of Crown Point Falls 2 miles from Rebel Camp.

A long, southwestward traverse and a few more switchbacks finally bring you to the meadow-bound shores of Lower Lyman Lake (5,598'). Campsites are located on the northern shore just as you approach the lake. You'll find additional sites off a spur trail on the west side of the lake that offer stunning views of Bonanza Peak.

If cascading creeks, opaque blue waters, a glacier-carved valley, and breathtaking alpine views interest you, make the 2-mile journey to the Upper Lyman Lakes. Evidence of retreating glaciers is right before your eyes as you hike over rocky moraines and circumnavigate tarns created by the ever-shrinking Lyman Glacier. You'll find great campsites with fantastic views of Chiwawa Mountain at the two upper lakes, but they afford limited shelter from the elements.

To continue on to the PCT, head northwest from Lower Lyman Lake, hiking about 2 miles to Cloudy Pass (6,438'). Even if you plan to do this hike as an out-and-back, it's worth hiking here for the views alone. The entire Agnes Creek valley stretches to the north, towering peaks and rugged ridges lining either side. A climb up Cloudy Peak wins views of the wild, rugged Glacier Peak.

To do this as a thru-hike to Stehekin, descend steeply to a junction with Suiattle Pass Trail. Take the hikers trail through steep boulders to reach Suiattle Pass. From there, head south on the PCT and follow the trail description for Agnes Creek (see next hike).

PERMIT INFORMATION Self-issued permits available at the trailhead.

DIRECTIONS From Seattle, drive east for 150 miles on US 2 over Stevens Pass to Wenatchee, and take the exit for Alt US 97 toward Rocky Reach Dam and Lake Chelan. The Lady of the Lake Ferry Terminal is on your left as you come into town, just past the sign marking the 30-mile-per-hour speed zone. It's a trip of about 2 hours on *Lady of the Lake II* to Lucerne. Verify pricing and schedules before you head out. From Lucerne, take the Holden shuttle 10 miles to Holden Village. Contact Holden Village to make shuttle reservations and verify times. (See Appendix A, page 221, for shuttle contact information.)

If you plan to do this as a thru-hike, take the bus from High Bridge Ranger Station (where you'll find schedules posted) to Stehekin. Catch *Lady of the Lake II* or the *Lady Express,* which is more expensive but much faster. Tickets can be purchased ahead of time or with cash or check at the dock.

GPS TRAILHEAD COORDINATES N48° 11.971' W120° 46.860'

27 Agnes Creek

SCENERY: ✿ ✿ ✿ ✿   TRAIL CONDITION: ✿ ✿ ✿

CHILDREN: ✿   DIFFICULTY: ✿ ✿ ✿

SOLITUDE: ✿ ✿ ✿ ✿   HIKING TIME: 3–5 days

DISTANCE: 38 miles out-and-back, 30 miles to Holden Village

GREEN TRAILS MAPS: *Holden 113 and McGregor Mountain 81*

OUTSTANDING FEATURES: Groves of beautiful cedar trees, alpine views, a peaceful boat ride on the third-deepest lake in the nation, and a chance to swing through the Stehekin Bakery

A 4-HOUR SCENIC BOAT RIDE up Lake Chelan to the small mountain town of Stehekin and an 11-mile bus ride that conveniently stops at the Stehekin Bakery eventually bring you to the trailhead. From there, the trail takes off up a long, remote valley to stunning high country and endless opportunities for exploration. Best of all, you can do this as a thru-hike by exiting through Railroad Creek to the Lutheran-based community of Holden Village, where you'll find showers and accommodation. Another 10-mile shuttle (or hike, if you're feeling really ambitious) brings you back to Lake Chelan.

🚶🚶 To get to the trailhead, take the Stehekin shuttle bus 11 miles to the High Bridge Ranger Station. Cross the bridge and, in about 500 feet, you reach the trailhead, on the left side of the road. Be sure to follow the signs for the southbound Pacific Crest Trail (PCT), and don't accidentally take Agnes Creek Gorge Trail.

From the trailhead, follow the PCT a short way down to Agnes Creek Gorge. You cross the creek on a wide, sturdy horse bridge that occasionally gets swept away by monster floods or damaged by falling trees. Before heading out, contact Stehekin Ranger Station to verify that the bridge is in place because fording it, even in late summer, is not the safest option.

Once you have crossed the creek, the trail makes its way up long switchbacks. In a little more than a mile, you reach a viewpoint that looks back

Agnes Creek

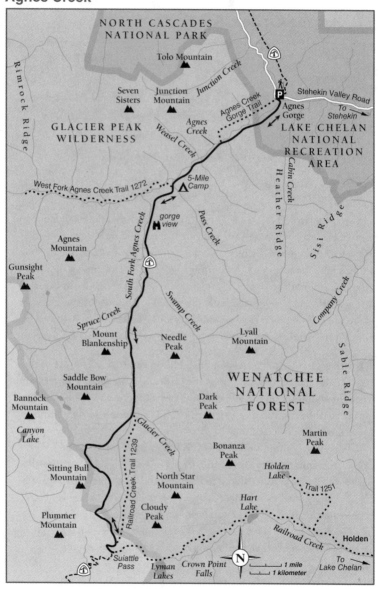

NORTH CASCADES NATIONAL PARK

Tolo Mountain ▲

Seven Sisters ▲

Junction Mountain ▲

Junction Creek

GLACIER PEAK WILDERNESS

Rimrock Ridge

Weasel Creek

Agnes Creek

Agnes Creek Gorge Trail

Stehekin Valley Road

Agnes Gorge

To Stehekin

LAKE CHELAN NATIONAL RECREATION AREA

West Fork Agnes Creek Trail 1272

5-Mile Camp

gorge view

Pass Creek

Cabin Creek

Heather Ridge

Sisi Ridge

Agnes Mountain ▲

Gunsight Peak ▲

South Fork Agnes Creek

Swamp Creek

Company Creek

Spruce Creek

Mount Blankenship ▲

Needle Peak ▲

Lyall Mountain ▲

WENATCHEE NATIONAL FOREST

Sable Ridge

Saddle Bow Mountain ▲

Bannock Mountain ▲

Canyon Lake

Dark Peak ▲

Glacier Creek

Railroad Creek Trail 1239

Sitting Bull Mountain ▲

North Star Mountain ▲

Bonanza Peak ▲

Martin Peak ▲

Holden Lake

Trail 1251

Plummer Mountain ▲

Cloudy Peak ▲

Hart Lake

Railroad Creek

Holden

Suiattle Pass

Lyman Lakes

Crown Point Falls

N

To Lake Chelan

1 mile
1 kilometer

toward Stehekin Valley and McGregor Mountain. A park service radio repeater shimmers in the sun just east of McGregor's summit.

In 0.5 mile, the trail exits Lake Chelan National Recreation Area and enters Glacier Peak Wilderness. The trail is fairly dull for the next 3.5 miles as it rolls through forested slopes to the junction with the West Fork of Agnes Creek Trail. This is also the site of 5-Mile Camp, a nice place to stop for the night if you head out on the same day you get dropped off by the ferry. The campsites are located among sparse timber just east of the trail on the west bank of Pass Creek.

Remain on the PCT as you leave 5-Mile Camp, and follow the trail along South Fork Agnes Creek. In 1.4 miles, you arrive at a viewpoint that will most likely exhaust your camera's battery. Precarious side trails take off from the main path and teeter on the edge of a deep gorge. Photo opportunities abound, and your gaze wanders up from the chaotic torrent toward the hard-to-access, rarely climbed giant known as Agnes Mountain. Beyond Agnes's rocky summit loom the distinct twin summits of Gunsight Peak.

After taking it all in, continue south on the PCT another 1.6 miles to Swamp Creek Camp. The camp, on the south side of Swamp Creek, is 100 yards or so downstream from the crossing. As you leave the site, you pass a sign for the unmaintained Swamp Creek Trail, which eventually reaches the Dark Glacier on the north side of Dark Peak and is likely a bushwhacking adventure through devil's club and alder.

The walking is pleasant for the next mile or so as the creek slips in and out of view. At one point, a massive logjam stretches from one bank to the

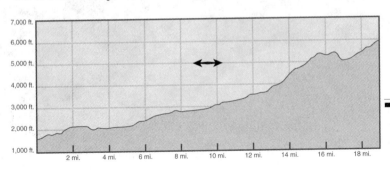

other, demonstrating just how powerful the water can be when the creeks are running high. A little way farther, you arrive at a hiker-only camp named Cedar, most likely for the beautiful western red cedars that dominate the forest. A level campsite sits on a knoll overlooking the creek. Water is easily accessible from camp.

For the next 0.5 mile, the trail parallels the creek. Along the way, it passes through thick forests of red cedar, Douglas-fir, hemlock, and spruce, then travels brushy avalanche slopes with open views of Mount Blankenship to the west and Needle Peak to the east.

At just more than 12 miles from the Stehekin Road, the trail arrives at Hemlock Camp, a great site along a tranquil section of the creek. Bear scat was prevalent in this area when I scouted this trip, so be sure to hang your food.

From here, the trail splits but eventually rejoins just below Suiattle Pass at South Fork Basin Camp. Railroad Creek Trail, which was the old PCT,

A marmot basks in the sun.

heads south up Agnes Creek about 5 miles, through a mix of brushy and forested slopes. You gain elevation gradually, and the scenery is similar to what you have already encountered. This is a good route for those hiking early in the season, when snow may be lingering up high.

The new PCT crosses Agnes Creek and takes a high route to South Fork Basin Camp. This route has a few more ups and downs and is about 1.5 miles longer than Railroad Creek Trail. If you plan to do this as a thru-hike to Holden Village, take the PCT's more challenging but much more rewarding high route.

Remaining on the PCT, cross Agnes on a footbridge and begin a steady 1,000-foot climb. Views to the south, toward Sitting Bull and North Star, unfold as you work your way into the high country. Approximately 1.5 miles from Hemlock, the trail ascends switchbacks next to a stream that pours steeply over polished slabs of bedrock, a good place to grab some water if you plan to stay at one of the sheltered camps in the Sitting Bull Basin.

The first of those camps is 0.5 mile or so from the creek. This hiker-only camp is tucked into a stand of trees that lies a few hundred yards off the trail. No fires are allowed, and water can be limited.

Continue along the trail as it heads west below Saddle Bow Mountain. Traverse a broad, flower-filled basin, where steep creeks and cascading water-falls tumble all around. The trail turns south, crosses a creek on a small bridge, and resumes a steady southeast climb to the heathery slopes below Sitting Bull. As the trail levels off, keep an eye out for a couple of designated campsites next to a small stream (5,400'). The views are spectacular, but the sites are exposed, so make sure the weather is decent if you plan to stay up there.

In 0.75 mile, the trail passes through a meadow strewn with boulders and clumps of dark, purple gentian. As you continue south, the trail descends more switchbacks to a second basin, below Plummer Mountain, with a much differ-ent character from the first one you entered. Gigantic boulders fill the upper basin, and the trail weaves and winds through these car-sized chunks of rock. As you climb back out—that's right, get ready for one more push!—Needle Peak and Dark Peak are visible in the distance to the northeast.

A mile from Plummer Basin and nearly 19 miles from the start of your journey, you reach the junction with Railroad Creek Trail 1256. To do this as

an out-and-back hike, descend east 0.25 mile into a small basin surrounded by talus slopes of white granite boulders and sheer rock cliffs. This is where you rejoin South Fork Agnes Creek. Descend north, and in 5 miles you arrive back at Hemlock Camp. From there, simply retrace your steps to Stehekin Road.

Those interested in hiking to Holden Village, continue south on the PCT to Suiattle Pass. From there head east along a precarious trail to Cloudy Pass. To continue to Holden Village, refer to the trail description for Lyman Lakes and Suiattle Pass (Hike 26, page 171).

PERMIT INFORMATION No permit required.

DIRECTIONS From Seattle, drive east for 150 miles on US 2 over Stevens Pass to Wenatchee, and take the exit for Alt US 97 toward Rocky Reach Dam and Lake Chelan. In 33 miles, the Lady of the Lake Ferry Terminal will be on your left as you come into town, just past the sign marking the 30-mile-per-hour speed zone. There are two ferry options to Stehekin: the *Lady of the Lake II* (4 hours) or the faster, more expensive *Lady Express* (2.5 hours). Verify pricing and schedules before you head out. From Stehekin, take the shuttle bus 11 miles to the High Bridge Ranger Station.

If you plan to do this as a thru-hike, take the shuttle bus 10 miles from Holden Village to the Lucerne boat landing. The ferry will pick you up on its return trip downvalley. Contact Holden Village for bus schedules and reservations. (See Appendix A, page 221, for shuttle contact information.)

GPS TRAILHEAD COORDINATES N48° 22.782' W120° 50.369'

OPPOSITE: *Descending into Plummer Basin*

28 Rainbow Lake and McAlester Creek

SCENERY: ✿ ✿ ✿ ✿ ✿   TRAIL CONDITION: ✿ ✿ ✿

CHILDREN: ✿ ✿   DIFFICULTY: ✿ ✿ ✿ ✿

SOLITUDE: ✿ ✿ ✿   DISTANCE: 31.5 miles

HIKING TIME: 3–5 days

GREEN TRAILS MAPS: *McGregor Mountain 81 and Stehekin 82*

OUTSTANDING FEATURES: Two tranquil alpine lakes; vistas of the rugged, glaciated peaks of the North Cascades; and a long loop hike into remote and wild country

UNLIKE MANY NATIONAL PARKS, North Cascades is not a park you can simply drive through to experience. There's no fancy visitor center to wander through or end-of-the-road extravaganza to snap pictures of. This park's true beauty is revealed only when you venture beyond the pavement and into the heart of the mountains. If you have never experienced the North Cascades, this hike is the perfect opportunity to do just that.

Quiet lakeside camping is just one of the highlights of this three-day hike.

From the parking area, find the narrow path that takes off from behind the information board in the far, eastern corner of the lot. Then, head south across WA 20 to pick up the main trail, on the other side of the road. The Pacific Crest Trail (PCT) is not far. Follow it south as it rolls gently through forested slopes 0.8 mile to the junction with Copper Pass/Stiletto Peak Trail. Stay on the PCT Bridge Creek Trail.

Just after the junction, the trail crosses Bridge Creek on a sturdy horse bridge. Beyond the crossing, views open to the east toward the Copper Creek drainage and Stiletto Peak (7,660'). The trail briefly reenters the forest and then crosses another open path at the 2-mile mark. A glance to the west reveals the lower slopes of Frisco Mountain (7,880') and the huge avalanche paths that stretch down to the valley below. If you hit this trail in early to mid-August, these paths are laden with an assortment of berries, including wild raspberries, thimbleberries, and huckleberries. It's no wonder bears are prevalent in this region.

A short distance from here is the U.S. Forest Service boundary. Another mile beyond that, the trail makes a slight turn to the west and, at 3.7 miles, arrives at the Twisp Pass junction. If you get a late start on the first day, you'll find a horse-and-hiker camp called Fireweed 0.1 mile to the east.

To continue toward Rainbow Lake remain on the southbound PCT. The trail turns due west and, at 4.3 miles, the sparkling glaciers of Mount Goode can be seen toward the head of the valley. In another 0.3 mile, the trail reaches Hideaway, a hiker-only camp tucked in a stand of tightly packed trees. The site, beside Bridge Creek, has space for two or three small tents. It's most likely buggy in the summer but is fine if you don't want to share a camp with horses.

Resume hiking on the PCT as the trail wanders in and out of slide paths. The hiking is fairly hot and dusty through this section; however, views south toward McGregor Mountain and the Sandalee Glacier make up for it. At this point, you can also see your route to Rainbow Lake via South Fork Bridge Creek.

At 6.3 miles, you reach the junction with South Fork Trail. Take this trail south as it descends steeply toward Bridge Creek. Follow the hiker signs, and

Rainbow Lake and McAlester Creek

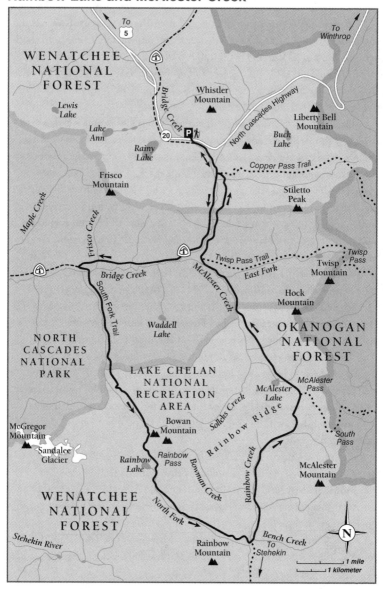

To 5

WENATCHEE NATIONAL FOREST

Lewis Lake

Lake Ann

Rainy Lake

Frisco Mountain

Maple Creek

Frisco Creek

Bridge Creek

Whistler Mountain

To Winthrop

North Cascades Highway

Liberty Bell Mountain

Buck Lake

Copper Pass Trail

Stiletto Peak

Twisp Pass Trail

East Fork

Twisp Pass

Twisp Mountain

McAlester Creek

Hock Mountain

OKANOGAN NATIONAL FOREST

NORTH CASCADES NATIONAL PARK

South Fork Trail

Waddell Lake

LAKE CHELAN NATIONAL RECREATION AREA

Soldits Creek

McAlester Lake

Rainbow Ridge

McAlester Pass

South Pass

McGregor Mountain

Sandalee Glacier

Bowan Mountain

Rainbow Lake

Rainbow Pass

Bowman Creek

Rainbow Creek

McAlester Mountain

WENATCHEE NATIONAL FOREST

Stehekin River

North Fork

Rainbow Mountain

Bench Creek To Stehekin

N

1 mile

1 kilometer

you soon reach a few large campsites, next to the creek (3,200'). There's no bridge at the crossing, so if you want to do this while the snow is still melting, check with a ranger station to see what conditions are like.

Once you have safely forded Bridge Creek, pick up the trail on the other side and climb steeply 0.5 mile through an old burn. The trail soon reenters the forest, and the gradient eases for the next 2 miles. Due to the remote nature of this trail, a couple seasons may go by without it being logged out. The year I hiked it, there were about a hundred downed trees that were easy to climb around but added a significant amount of hiking time. Be sure to check the latest trail conditions before you head out.

As you slowly work your way upvalley, McGregor and Bowan Mountains occasionally come into view. At 8.8 miles, the trail reaches Dan's Camp, a hiker-only campsite with space for one or two tents—not my first choice, but if South Fork is full or you're looking for solitude, it'll work.

At 9 miles, you reach Lake Chelan National Recreation Area. Just beyond the boundary, the trail travels 100 yards or so up a meadow to offer a great view of Bowan Mountain.

As you reenter the forest, get ready to climb. See all those squiggle marks on the Green Trails map? That's right, those are tight switchbacks that take you more than 500 feet in 0.5 mile. When the trail reaches 4,800 feet, the incline eases and the north basin of McGregor Mountain comes into full view. The scene is spectacular, with water from the Sandalee Glacier forming creeks that cascade into the valley below.

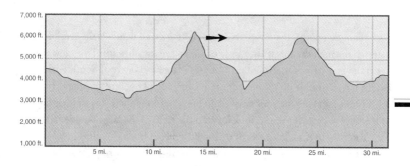

Rainbow Lake

From this point, the temperature cools as the trail parallels the creek for a stretch through the forest. In 1 mile or so, you reach a beautiful meadow that lies at the base of Bowan Mountain (7,895'). The headwaters of South Fork Bridge Creek tumble down the mountain's rocky flanks before snaking through the meadow, making the trail mucky and fairly hard to follow. If you lose the trail after you cross the creek, look for it to the right of the large boulder field.

You now begin a long ascent through stands of larch, hemlock, and alpine fir. This slope can hold snow well into July and may require an ice axe.

After a fairly long, steady climb, the trail eventually tops out at Rainbow Pass (6,200'). Rainbow Lake can be seen 600 feet below in an amphitheater of polished rock walls. Beyond the lake, impressive vistas stretch out to the south toward the two-pronged summit of Tupshin Peak (8,100') and White Goat Mountain (7,820'). Immediately to the east lies Bowan's summit. Unfortunately, the rock is crumbly and very unappealing to climb. If you're looking to do a little cross-country exploration before you descend to the lake, a ridge stretching to the west toward McGregor Mountain could be worth venturing out on.

To continue to the lake, descend south from the pass until you reach a spur trail that takes you to the eastern shoreline. Excellent campsites are located on a bench just above the lake, and in the evening, alpenglow dances on the summits and ridgelines that surround it. There are only four sites, and they fill quickly, so try to get a backcountry permit early to secure a spot.

From the lake, the trail takes a high route and offers up a panoramic view to the southwest toward the glaciated north face of Dark Peak (8,504'). A series of tiered, rocky switchbacks descends 500 feet to a forested path. Just before the trail exits the forest and enters the flowery fields of Rainbow Meadows, you see a sign for Rainbow Meadows Group Camp, which offers quick, easy access to the meadow. The campground is tucked into a stand of trees in another 0.25 mile, and the standard sites are at the southern end of the meadow in thick timber, a short distance off the trail.

The next 3 miles travel through a mix of forested and open slopes, offering plenty of opportunities to check out the surrounding peaks and valleys. Around the 19-mile mark, the trail crosses Rainbow Creek on a foot log and climbs 250 feet to the Rainbow Creek Trail junction. Head north up the Rainbow Creek drainage toward McAlester Pass. Heading south on this trail takes you to the small boat-access town of Stehekin (see Hikes 26 and 27 for more information).

A nice little camp called Bench Creek is just beyond the junction. In another 1.5 miles, Bowan Mountain peeks out once again, and in 0.3 mile, you arrive at the hiker-only Bowan Camp, which is just off the trail and has year-round water access from Rainbow Creek.

In another mile, the trail boulder-hops across Rainbow Creek once again. From the crossing, the path climbs a couple switchbacks to pop out below Rainbow Ridge. The entire valley stretches to the north and, for the first time, McAlester Pass comes into view.

The next 0.5 mile is fairly flat and remains in the cool shade of the forest. As the trail begins its climb, you get a great opportunity to take photos of McAlester Mountain, at 5,600 feet. One final push brings you to the subalpine meadows of McAlester Pass (6,000') where exploration opportunities abound. One great option is to hike 1.4 miles to South Pass and wander the high country that extends in either direction.

If you're looking for solitude, a one-site, hiker-only camp is located on the north side of the meadow. Once the water dries up in the meadow, though, it's a 0.5-mile walk toward McAlester Lake or Hidden Meadows Horse Camp to get water.

To continue to the lake, head northwest, descending 500 feet in less than 1 mile to a spur trail for McAlester Lake. Follow the hiker signs to find the numerous campsites scattered along the north side of the lake. This is one of the more popular lakes in the area because of the great fishing, easy horse access, and relative proximity to the North Cascades Highway. That said, it's still worth spending a night at this tranquil little lake. If there's no room or you're continuing on, there's a great grassy meadow to eat lunch in just outside the hiker campsites.

Walking is enjoyable for the next 3 miles as you descend into the McAlester Creek drainage. A half mile beyond the national park boundary, the trail crosses the East Fork of McAlester, a potentially hazardous crossing early in the season. In another 0.5 mile, you reach the junction with Twisp Pass. Remain on McAlester Creek Trail.

The last campsite on this 30-mile loop is just past the junction. Fireweed Camp is a hiker-and-horse camp on McAlester Creek, the same campsite mentioned earlier as a great place to break up the first or last day of your trip. Two hiker sites have space for up to 12 people.

From camp, follow the trail as it crosses just below the confluence of McAlester and Bridge Creeks. A few hundred feet beyond the crossing, the trail rejoins the PCT. Follow that north 3.7 miles to the start of your hike at the Bridge Creek Trailhead.

PERMIT INFORMATION Northwest Forest Pass ($30/year) required; see tinyurl.com/northwestforestpass for more information. Back-country permits must be obtained in person on the first day or up to one day before your backpacking trip on a first-come, first-served basis. Permits are available at the Wilderness Information Center in Marblemount or the USFS ranger stations in Chelan or Winthrop. (See Appendix A, page 221, for contact information.)

DIRECTIONS From Seattle, take I-5 north about 65 miles to Exit 230 and turn right (east) on WA 20. As you head toward North Cascades National Park, note that services are limited east of Concrete, about 30 miles east of Exit 230, so this is your best bet for shopping for food or getting gas. Drive 51 miles past Marblemount to Rainy Pass. Continue east another mile and look for a large parking area, called Bridge Creek, on the north side of the highway. If you're coming from the east, the Bridge Creek Trailhead is about 34 miles from Winthrop, on the north side of the highway.

GPS TRAILHEAD COORDINATES N48° 30.273' W120° 43.030'

29 Cutthroat Pass

SCENERY: ✿ ✿ ✿ ✿ ✿

CHILDREN: ✿ ✿ ✿

SOLITUDE: ✿ ✿

HIKING TIME: 5–7 hours

TRAIL CONDITION: ✿ ✿ ✿ ✿ ✿

DIFFICULTY: ✿ ✿ ✿

DISTANCE: 10 miles

GREEN TRAILS MAP: *Washington Pass 50*

OUTSTANDING FEATURES: Grand vistas of snowcapped mountains and weather-worn peaks, a gradual ascent on a well-maintained trail, and plenty of opportunities to extend your hike once you reach the pass

WHILE RESEARCHING THE TRAILS FOR this book, I ran into a gardener from Stehekin who set out to hike the entire Pacific Crest Trail (PCT) in the 1970s. He made it all the way to southern Oregon. When I asked why he didn't keep going, he simply said, "Well, the Pasayten Wilderness was just too beautiful to leave." He hitched a ride back north and hasn't left since. While Cutthroat Pass is not part of Pasayten Wilderness or North Cascades National Park, many believe it should be. Since it's not, however, dog lovers can bring their canine companions.

A sign clearly marks the start of the trail.

Unlike most hikes in the North Cascades, this one begins with a warm-up. The trail is mostly flat for the first 0.25 mile as it travels north through a forest thick with fir, hemlock, and spruce. You hike a few long, leisurely switchbacks before the trail levels out. At the 1-mile mark, a rock offers a place to sit and enjoy excellent views to the southwest toward Corteo Peak. Views open to the west as well, but the trail soon reenters the forest, obscuring the vista.

Walking is pleasant as the trail continues its journey north up the Porcupine Creek drainage. At 2 miles, you cross the creek on a footbridge, after which the trail begins a gradual climb to the northeast. In a little less than 1 mile, there's a small campsite beside the trail, a great spot if the weather is bad, but the camping up higher is much more beautiful.

At 3.2 miles, the trail transitions from dark, forested slopes to open meadows littered with wildflowers. Views open in all directions, and for the first time you can see Cutthroat Pass at the head of the valley to the northeast. The trail quickly reenters a short section of trees before immersing you in spectacular alpine terrain.

The trail rounds the head of the valley and at 4 miles comes to the best camping in the area. A sign directs hikers to three or four sites that have access to a few small springs, a good place to refill water bottles or let thirsty dogs grab a drink before your final climb to the pass, where water is absent unless snowfields linger.

From here, the trail begins a long series of switchbacks. As you wind up the east side of the valley, Peaks 7004 and 7726, to the west, rise steeply above the path you took to get here. The vegetation takes on a scrubbier appearance; harsh winds and fierce storms permit only the strongest of plants to survive. Larch trees, low-lying huckleberry bushes, and heather soon dominate the landscape.

Cutthroat Pass (6,820') is at 5 miles, and vistas open in all directions. Tower Mountain is directly north, Cutthroat Peak's rocky summit lies to the south, Silver Star dominates views to the east, and the dark-colored rock of Black Peak can be seen to the west.

And that's just the beginning. If time and energy permit, there's still a ton of exploring to do. Cross-country travelers can venture out on a number

Cutthroat Pass

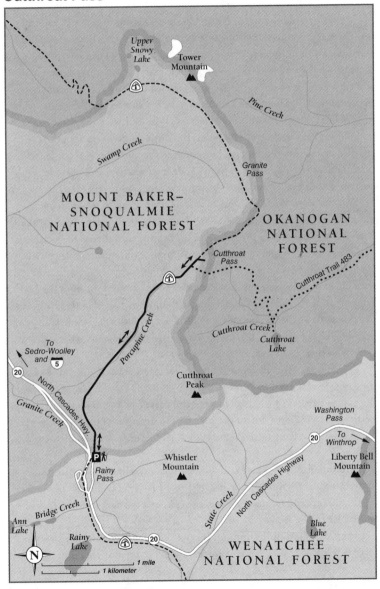

of spur trails from the pass. You can also continue another mile north on the PCT to Granite Pass (6,290'), where you'll be rewarded once again with breathtaking views of the North Cascades and Pasayten Wilderness.

Not feeling ambitious? Don't worry: a large rock, with room for two, is conveniently located at the pass for your lounging pleasure. The rock has been worn white from years of use by marmots and mountain folk basking in its warmth in the late afternoon sun.

If you want to spend the night, there are a couple of sites at the pass itself. Be aware that there's no water here once the snow is gone and very limited protection from the elements; storms can roll through without warning. If there's any chance of poor weather, it's probably best to spend the day exploring the pass and the evening hunkered down in the shelter of the campsites you passed on the way up.

To return, simply retrace your steps, or, if you can arrange to swap keys with another hiking party, you can do a thru-hike by descending to Cutthroat Lake via Trail 483. The trail branches off from the PCT just north of Cutthroat Pass; Cutthroat Lake is about 3.5 miles on. From the lake, it's another 2 miles to the trailhead.

PERMIT INFORMATION Northwest Forest Pass ($30/year) required; see tinyurl.com/northwestforestpass for more information. Self-issued permits available at the trailhead.

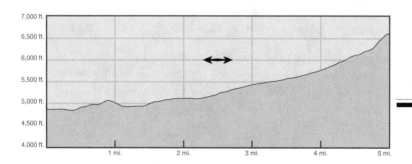

Looking north from Cutthroat Pass   PHOTO: JEN SCHUMACHER

DIRECTIONS

FROM SEATTLE: From Seattle, take I-5 north about 65 miles to Exit 230 and turn right (east) on WA 20. As you head toward North Cascades National Park, note that services are limited east of Concrete, about 30 miles east of Exit 230, so this is your best bet for shopping for food or getting gas. Drive 51 miles past Marblemount to Rainy Pass; if you're coming from the east, Rainy Pass is approximately 35 miles from Winthrop. Turn north off of WA 20, following signs for the northbound PCT. The road ends in 0.25 mile, at the trailhead parking lot. The trail, clearly signed, is in the back left (north) corner of the parking lot.

TO CUTTHROAT LAKE TRAIL 483: Continue east on WA 20 from Rainy Pass. Turn left (west) about 4.5 miles from Washington Pass onto Cutthroat Creek Road (Spur Road 400), and drive a little more than a mile to the road's end. The trailhead is at the end of the road.

GPS TRAILHEAD COORDINATES N48° 33.347' W120° 39.344'

30 Grasshopper Pass

SCENERY: ✿ ✿ ✿ ✿

CHILDREN: ✿ ✿ ✿ ✿

SOLITUDE: ✿ ✿

HIKING TIME: 4–6 hours

TRAIL CONDITION: ✿ ✿ ✿ ✿ ✿

DIFFICULTY: ✿ ✿

DISTANCE: 11 miles

GREEN TRAILS MAP: *Washington Pass 50*

OUTSTANDING FEATURES: Golden larch trees in the fall, abundant wildflowers in the summer, and a 360-degree view of the North Cascades for the entire hike

THIS HIKE'S GREAT FEATURES SHOULD convince you to plan to spend your next vacation in the Methow Valley. For starters, the drive to the trailhead takes you by the Mazama Store, one of my favorite places to stop for a coffee and a berry scone. The U.S. Forest Service road is enough beauty for most people, as it steadily climbs through alpine terrain to an elevation of 6,400 feet. Everything beyond the trailhead feels like a bonus as you hike in awe of the grand views surrounding you. The best time to hike it is in fall, when the larches turn a bright, golden yellow. Regardless of when you go, make sure to check the weather before you head out. The trail travels above treeline and offers minimal (if any) protection from nasty weather.

🚶🚶 To begin this hike, you can either continue on the main road (FR 5400) past Meadows Campground to Harts Pass and the Pacific Crest Trail (PCT) trailhead—a good option to extend your hike, as it adds 4 miles to an already lengthy day—or you can save some energy to explore the terrain that awaits you by beginning 2 miles south of Harts Pass at Meadows Campground. The trail takes off from the far right corner of the parking lot, and a short, steep pitch quickly brings you to the PCT.

Head south on the PCT across an open scree slope below the abandoned Brown Bear Mine. The trail gently climbs to a broad shoulder offering excellent views south and southeast into Trout Creek. As you look across the valley, note the stands of snags and remnants of burnt trees, similar to those you drove through to get here. They were all damaged in the Needle Fire, which

Grasshopper Pass

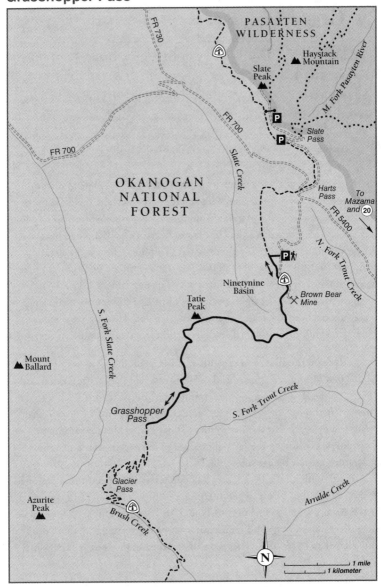

PASAYTEN WILDERNESS

FR 730

FR 700

FR 700

Slate Creek

Haystack Mountain

Slate Peak

Slate Pass

M. Fork Pasayten River

Harts Pass

To Mazama and 20

FR 5400

N. Fork Trout Creek

OKANOGAN NATIONAL FOREST

Ninetynine Basin

Tatie Peak

Brown Bear Mine

S. Fork Slate Creek

Mount Ballard

S. Fork Trout Creek

Grasshopper Pass

Glacier Pass

Azurite Peak

Brush Creek

Arralde Creek

N

1 mile

1 kilometer

swept through this area back in 2003, burning thousands of acres of federal, state, and private land.

From here, the trail curves to the west and follows a gentle gradient through stands of larches, mountain hemlock, and western white pines to a windswept saddle at 7,000 feet. Views open in just about every direction, with Ninetynine Basin and the Slate Peak Lookout to the north, Tatie Peak to the west, and a sea of rugged peaks to the south. If the views still aren't enough, a short, easy scramble westward will lead you to the 7,386-foot summit of Tatie Peak.

The trail travels below Tatie Peak to another saddle, from which you can see the glaciated slopes of Crater Mountain off to the northwest. From the saddle, cross the head of a feeder stream to the South Fork of Trout Creek and immediately enter a stand of larches. Descend a couple of lazy switchbacks to a long path that arrives at a forested bench, 4 miles from the trailhead. Enjoy a picnic in the shadow of Mount Ballard or spend the night at one of a few fairly protected campsites nestled among the trees (water is available from a small stream to the south).

To continue your journey, remain on the PCT as it heads south another mile to Grasshopper Pass (6,700'). Just beyond the pass, the PCT drops steeply to the broad, forested saddle of Glacier Pass. If you have extra energy, continue on a narrow path that heads south from the pass out the ridge. Ascend a knob, and remain on the trail as it follows the ridgeline through scrubby trees and rocky terrain to Point 7125. Views from here are

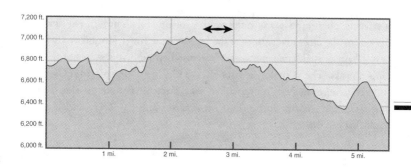

Azurite Peak rises dramatically above the trail.

spectacular, to say the least. To the south, Golden Horn's prominent summit sits among the craggy ridgelines of the Needles and Tower Mountain. To the west is Azurite Peak's enormous east face, and beyond that lies a sea of snow-capped peaks. The 360-degree vista offers a bird's-eye view of Trout Creek and a number of named and unnamed peaks stretching out to the east. To the north, you can see your entire route weave across hillsides, over saddles, and finally back to the trailhead.

PERMIT INFORMATION Northwest Forest Pass ($30/year) required; see tinyurl.com/northwestforestpass for more information. Self-issued permits available at the trailhead.

DIRECTIONS From Seattle, take I-5 north about 65 miles to Exit 230 and turn right (east) on WA 20. As you head toward North Cascades National Park, note that services are limited east of Concrete, about 30 miles east of Exit 230, so this is your best bet for shopping for food or getting gas. The town of Mazama is on the east side of Washington Pass, about 120 miles east of Exit 230 and 1.5 miles past Early Winters Campground. Turn left (north) off WA 20 onto Lost River Road. Proceed to the T-intersection and turn left (west), remaining on Lost River Road. From here, it's 18.5 miles to Harts Pass.

The road begins on pavement but soon turns into washboard gravel when it becomes Forest Road 5400, a one-lane road with pullouts and an infamous stretch that will turn your knuckles white. Needless to say, use caution and drive slowly. As you approach Harts Pass, keep an eye out for Meadows Campground. Turn left (south) and drive 2 miles, past Meadows Campground, to the road's end.

GPS TRAILHEAD COORDINATES N48° 42.620' W120° 40.600'

31 | Tamarack Peak

SCENERY: ✿✿✿✿✿	TRAIL CONDITION: ✿✿✿✿
CHILDREN: ✿✿✿✿	DIFFICULTY: ✿✿
SOLITUDE: ✿✿	DISTANCE: 8–10 miles
HIKING TIME: 5–7 hours	GREEN TRAILS MAP: *Pasayten Peak 18*

OUTSTANDING FEATURES: Interesting history, gorgeous alpine vistas, and brilliant colors in the fall

UNLIKE MANY TRAILS ALONG THE Pacific Crest Trail (PCT), this route remains on the crest throughout the entire hike. The trail starts at 6,800 feet and travels through some of Washington's most wild high country, where rare species, including lynx, wolves, grizzly bears, and wolverines, have been making a strong comeback. In the fall, larch trees turn a golden yellow, providing a stark contrast to the vibrant red that covers the hillsides.

Tamarack Peak

🚶🚶 To begin your day exploring Pasayten Wilderness, drive 1.5 miles past the trailhead to the end of the road for a short side hike to the Slate Peak Lookout. At 7,488 feet, it's the highest lookout in the state you can drive to. Although the lookout itself is off-limits, you still get a 360-degree view of the North Cascades, and helpful diagrams in every corner help you identify some of the notable peaks.

Another of the lookout's draws is its intriguing history, dating back to the mid-1900s. When the U.S. Forest Service first used this site as a fire lookout, access was via a steep, rocky trail that ran from Harts Pass to the top of the peak. In the 1950s, the Cold War brought the U.S. Air Force into the region, and Slate Peak was designated the perfect spot from which to detect enemy planes. Soon a road was built, the old lookout was removed, and the top of Slate Peak was blasted off! Construction on the radar station began, but, before it was finished, the project was declared obsolete. The land was given back to the U.S. Forest Service, and another fire lookout was built on top of the abandoned station. The top of the lookout now stands as tall as the original Slate Peak summit.

When you have had your fill of stunning views and local history here, head back down the road to the PCT trailhead (6,800'). From the parking lot, follow the trail north as it wraps around the west side of Slate Peak. Looking west, you can see a large scar in a hillside just below your objective, Tamarack Peak. This is the site of an old gold mine known as "The Glory Hole" that brought prospectors to the area back in 1894. Men traveled from all over and lived in the small mining town of Barron, working for a meager $2.50 per day plus meals. Most men never realized their dreams, and after two years, the veins of gold disappeared underground where it was too costly to extract them. Barron became a ghost town, and over the next 40 years, a few mines came and went. Today, much of the land is still privately held, and a few people still come to prospect.

Beyond the Glory Hole, Crater and Jack Mountains shimmer in the afternoon sun; nestled between them, far off in the distance, rises Mount Baker and Mount Shuksan. Near 2 miles, the trail rounds a grassy shoulder and makes a slow descent into a basin just above Benson Creek Camp. From

Tamarack Peak

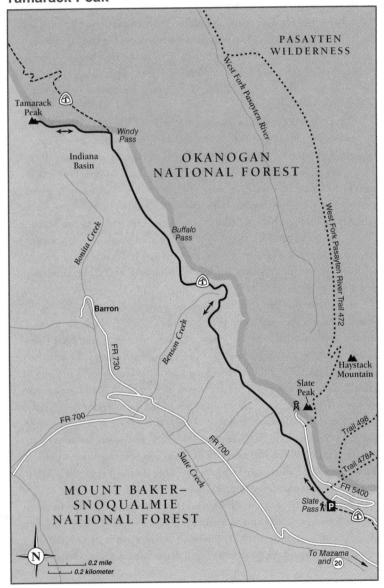

a small pass, views open to the north toward the Pasayten River, Gold Ridge, and Pasayten Peak.

From here, the trail bears west, contouring around an arm before resuming its northward trajectory. Along the way, you pass through semiforested slopes of alpine fir and larch (also known as tamarack). In the fall, the hillsides in this area are a spectacle of vibrant colors, from the bright-yellow needles of the larches to the deep-red hues of low-lying huckleberry bushes.

Three miles from the trailhead, you arrive at Buffalo Pass (6,550'). Follow the PCT another mile, to the broad, sparsely forested Windy Pass (6,257'). For many people, especially those with kids, this is a great spot to enjoy lunch and call it a day. If you still have energy, explore cross-country to the top of Tamarack Peak, but be prepared to do some route finding and a bit of steep traversing along the way.

From the pass, head west up a wide ridge that comes off the east side of Tamarack. Ascend through heather slopes—slick when wet!—to the ridge proper. Around 6,800 feet, you enter Pasayten Wilderness, which at the time of this writing was marked by a random bright-orange sign in the middle of the slope. Game trails lead the way until the ridge narrows and you're forced to push your way through scrub trees onto the south face. When the opportunity arises (around 6,900'), work your way back onto the ridge, which has broadened by this point. From here, it's an easy walk to the 7,290-foot summit of Tamarack Peak, where you'll most likely enjoy the panoramic views alone.

To the south lies a sea of peaks, including Silver Star, the Needles, Golden Horn, Azurite, and Ballard. Several glaciated peaks, including Mount Baker

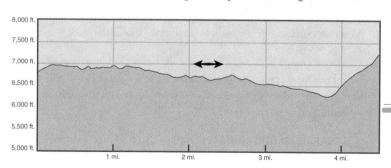

and Snowfield Peak, shine far in the distance to the west and southwest. The rain shadow effect can be seen in the dry rugged mountains that stretch to the east; to the north, the PCT stretches another 25 miles to the Canadian border through some of Washington's most wild and desolate country.

PERMIT INFORMATION Northwest Forest Pass ($30/year) required; see tinyurl.com/northwestforestpass for more information. Self-issued permits available at the trailhead.

DIRECTIONS

FROM SEATTLE: Take I-5 north about 65 miles to Exit 230 and turn right (east) on WA 20. As you head toward North Cascades National Park, note that services are limited east of Concrete, about 30 miles east of Exit 230, so this is your best bet for shopping for food or getting gas. The town of Mazama is on the east side of Washington Pass, about 120 miles east of Exit 230 and 1.5 miles past Early Winters Campground. Turn left (north) off WA 20, onto Lost River Road. Proceed to the T-intersection and turn left (west), onto Okanogan County Road 9140. From here, it's 18.5 miles to Harts Pass.

The road begins on pavement but soon turns into washboard gravel when it becomes Forest Road 5400, a one-lane road with pull-outs and an infamous stretch that will turn your knuckles white. Needless to say, use caution and drive slowly. When you arrive at Harts Pass, bear right onto the 3-mile-long Slate Peak Road (FR 5400-600). At 1.5 miles, the road makes a tight switchback. Park on the small shoulder on the outside bend. There is parking for six to eight cars. If no spaces are available, there's room to park on the side of the road.

TO SLATE PEAK LOOKOUT: From the PCT trailhead, continue up Slate Peak Road, past another switchback and the Slate Pass Trailhead, to a permanently closed gate. It's 0.25 mile and 200 feet of elevation gain to the lookout.

GPS TRAILHEAD COORDINATES N48° 43.941' W120° 40.538'

32 West Fork Pasayten to PCT

SCENERY: ✿ ✿ ✿ ✿	TRAIL CONDITION: ✿ ✿ ✿
CHILDREN: ✿ ✿	DIFFICULTY: ✿ ✿ ✿ ✿
SOLITUDE: ✿ ✿ ✿	DISTANCE: 22.5 miles
HIKING TIME: 2–3 days	GREEN TRAILS MAP: *Pasayten Peak 18*

OUTSTANDING FEATURES: Travels through moose, grey wolf, and lynx habitat, stunning alpine campsites, and one of the best high routes in Washington

THIS HIKE COULD REALLY BE divided into two sections. The West Fork of the Pasayten is a rugged, mostly wooded hike that ambles along the river, with few people and abundant wildlife. The PCT is a very popular, well-maintained high route with stunning views and spectacular camping options. This would probably be a more popular loop hike; however, at the time of this writing, the U.S. Forest Service had not maintained the West Fork Trail in two years. Be sure to check trail conditions before heading out.

🚶🚶 This hike begins with a short, stout climb up the road toward Slate Peak Lookout. As you grind your way up, you can catch a glimpse of your return route on the Pacific Crest Trail (PCT) as it cuts through the hillside just below the road. The trailhead is reached in a quarter mile. For those who have never been to the lookout, it's worth dropping your pack here and climbing the last little bit to the tower. A full description and the history of Slate Peak can be found at the beginning of the Tamarack Peak hike (Hike 31, page 202).

From the road, the trail heads north, descending through a spectacular flower-filled bowl. Views are stunning in every direction as you leave the trailhead. Gold Ridge and Pasayten Peak (7,850') rise to the east, and the broad, forested drainage of the West Fork of the Pasayten River stretches north on its journey from Canada's Similkameen River. As you work your way down the bowl, be sure to look back up toward Slate Peak Lookout looming overhead.

Descending, the trail takes on a more subalpine feel as it winds its way through stands of larches and mountain hemlock. At 2.7 miles, the trail finally leaves the alpine altogether and enters the forest. The next mile is

West Fork Pasayten to PCT

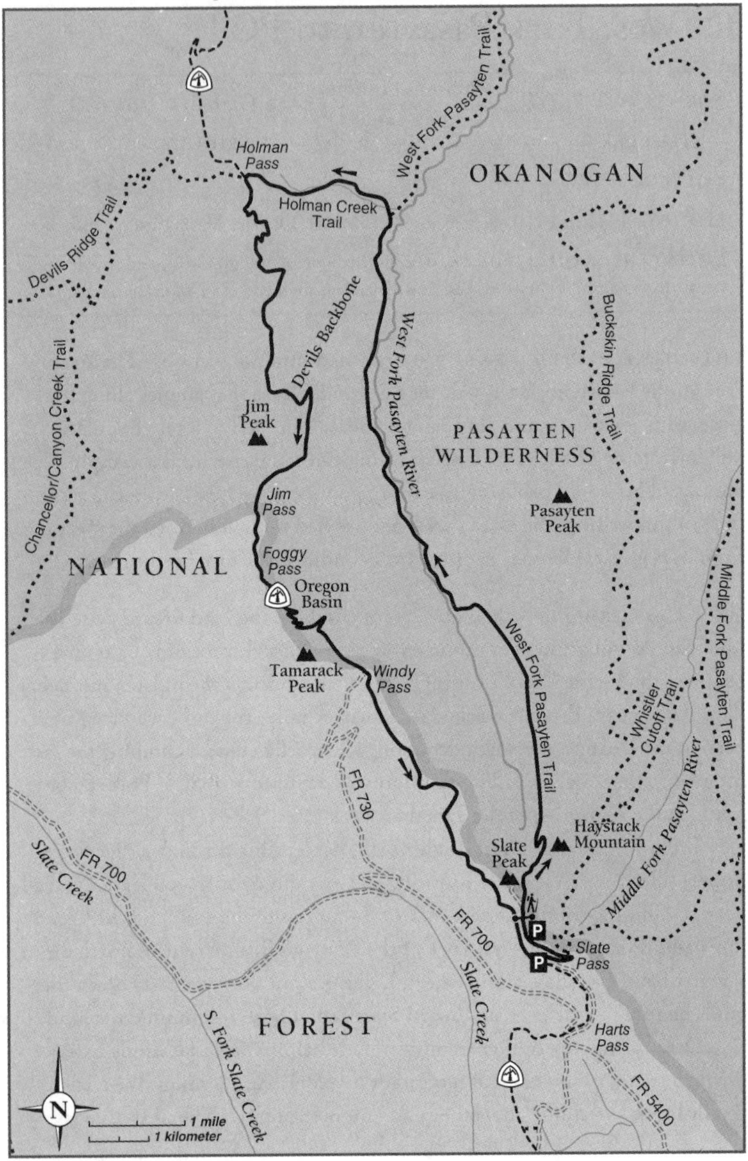

Holman Pass

Holman Creek Trail

West Fork Pasayten Trail

OKANOGAN

Devils Ridge Trail

Devils Backbone

Jim Peak

Jim Pass

Foggy Pass

Oregon Basin

Chancellor/Canyon Creek Trail

West Fork Pasayten River

PASAYTEN WILDERNESS

Pasayten Peak

Buckskin Ridge Trail

NATIONAL

Tamarack Peak

Windy Pass

West Fork Pasayten Trail

Whistler Cutoff Trail

Middle Fork Pasayten Trail

Haystack Mountain

Slate Peak

Middle Fork Pasayten River

FR 790

FR 700

Slate Creek

P

P

Slate Pass

FR 700

Slate Creek

S. Fork Slate Creek

FOREST

Harts Pass

FR 5400

N

1 mile
1 kilometer

relatively uneventful as the trail continues a gradual descent, traversing through meadows along the western flank of Gold Ridge.

At 3.8 miles, the trail makes a quick descent toward the river, and it's here that trail conditions begin to change. The half mile to the river is rutted out and slick, with water running directly down the trail in many places. Remnants of an old boardwalk can be seen piled along the edge of the trail for the next mile or so. It becomes obvious why the boardwalk was needed (lack of funding required the U.S. Forest Service to remove it), as most of the trail along the West Fork is fairly muddy and waterlogged. By August, it's relatively easy to keep your feet dry along these areas.

At 4.2 miles, the trail arrives at its first camp. It's a decent camp, but it's worth hiking another half mile to a lovely little camp that lies along the river near an open meadow. This camp is a great option if you only have a half day and want to get settled in along the trail. The bugs along the river can be horrendous, so be prepared. With that said, camping out is probably your best bet for seeing the abundant wildlife.

Continuing on, the trail crosses the river at the 5-mile mark. By August, it's easy to rock-hop or wade through ankle-deep water. A camp lies on the other side that some maps note as Lid Kay Camp. The site is fairly unremarkable, with a better, more established camp a half mile farther down the trail.

The trail crosses Oregon Creek (which drains from the Oregon Basin, a great spot to camp along the PCT) at 6.3 miles. There is a small site for one tent right on the creek. From the creek, the trail travels along the river, passing

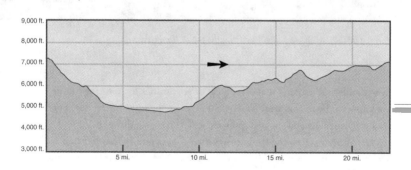

Rugged peaks rise in every direction from the top of Jim Peak.

by wetlands and marshes that offer great opportunities for spotting moose that
are known to be in this area. The next 2 miles are brushy and muddy, but the
trail is mostly flat, and the bad spots are easy to navigate through.

Around 8 miles, the trail crosses Shaw Creek and in another half mile
arrives at the junction for Holman Pass Trail 472A. The West Fork Trail

continues north, heading deep into the heart of the Pasayten Wilderness. Head west toward Holman Pass and the PCT.

The trail crosses another creek a short distance from the junction and arrives at a large camp on the far side of the crossing. Be sure to fill up water bottles before continuing on, as it's the last good, reliable water source for the next 6 miles. From the creek, the trail begins a gradual climb, and in another 1.5 miles arrives at the forested slopes of Holman Pass (5,100'). The pass itself is fairly unremarkable, mostly forested with no views, but it does mark the turning point of this hike. After thrashing my way down the West Fork of the Pasayten, I have to admit arriving at the PCT was a bit of a shock. I saw four different parties in the 10 minutes I sat at Holman Pass (after having seen only one on the entire West Fork Trail), and I was pleasantly surprised at how pristinely maintained the trail was.

Besides the amount of people and the change in trail conditions, the environment that the trail travels through also takes on a completely new feel. As you work your way up from the pass, the trail soon enters the subalpine and amazingly remains in it for the entire hike back to Slate Pass. As views open to the north toward Holman Peak (7,550') and Shull Mountain (7,830'), it becomes obvious why this section of the PCT has become so popular over the years.

At 13.4 miles, the trail arrives at a campsite with a seasonal water supply and room for one to two small tents. In another mile, views open up toward the long arm of Devils Backbone and the north side of Jim Peak. In a short distance, the trail arrives at Shaw Creek. If you're planning on camping at Devils Backbone, be sure to fill up here, as this is the main water source, and it's another mile and 300 feet of elevation gain to camp. There's a small creek in the next basin over, but in most years it would be dry by fall.

If camping at Devils Backbone on a weekend, be sure to get there early, as it's one of the more popular campsites in this area. There are three sites on the ridge, two on the northern end of the ridge and one right next to the trail. If all three of these sites are full, a grassy area at the base of Jim Peak has room for one to two small tents. Even if you don't end up camping here, a scramble up Jim Peak (7,033') is well worth the effort. A climbers' trail can be located on the opposite side of the PCT from the campsites on Devils Backbone. The route consists of mostly steep heather and occasional Class 3 climbing. Once you reach the top, views of the North Cascades are stunning in every direction.

Leaving camp, the trail stays mostly level as it traverses below the southern end of Devils Backbone with stunning views into the West Fork of the Pasayten and occasional glimpses north toward Mount Ballard (8,340'). At 16.4 miles, the trail arrives at Jim Pass. A grassy site lies to the west of the trail; however, a more private campsite can be found below the pass in Oregon Basin. The trail branches to the east and descends through a meadow to a stand of trees. Water can be limited in this area, so make sure you have plenty if you're going to camp here.

From Jim Pass, the trail wraps around the west side of a knoll and in another mile crosses back to the east at Foggy Pass. The trail begins a long, gradual climb, passing a camp at the headwaters of Oregon Creek. At 18 miles, you arrive at a spectacular saddle (6,700') that lies at the base of Tamarack Peak (7,290').

Better camping, with a more consistent water source, can be found after descending a couple switchbacks to the basin below the saddle. There are two sites, the first lying just off the main trail. The more private of the two can be found a short distance farther on a spur trail that branches off to the right. From the basin, it's a short climb to Windy Pass and the Pasayten Wilderness boundary.

For a detailed description of Windy Pass to the PCT trailhead, please see the description for Tamarack Peak (Hike 31, page 202). In summary, it's a 4-mile high route through picturesque meadows to the trailhead. I opted to drop my pack here for the 1-mile hike back to the car. If you're lucky, you may even be able to hitch a ride from someone heading up to Slate Peak.

PERMIT INFORMATION Northwest Forest Pass ($30/year) required; see tinyurl.com/northwestforestpass for more information. Self-issued permits available at the trailhead.

DIRECTIONS

From Seattle, take I-5 north about 65 miles to Exit 230 and turn right (east) on WA 20. As you head toward North Cascades National Park, note that services are limited east of Concrete, about 30 miles east of Exit 230, so this is your best bet for shopping for food or getting gas.

The town of Mazama is on the east side of Washington Pass, about 120 miles east of Exit 230 and 1.5 miles past Early Winters Campground. The "town" consists of a gear shop, Goat's Beard Mountain Supplies, and the Mazama Store, which is a great little grocery store–bakery. Both of these places are good options for information or if you forget any last-minute items. To get to Mazama, turn left (north) off WA 20 onto Lost River Road. At the T-intersection, turn left onto Okanogan County Road 9140. Both stores are on the right side of the road (Goat's Beard is behind the Mazama Store).

From Mazama, it's 18.5 miles west on Okanogan County Road 9140 to Harts Pass. The road begins on pavement but soon turns into washboard gravel when it becomes Forest Road 5400, a one-lane with pullouts and an infamous stretch that will turn your knuckles white. Needless to say, use caution and drive slowly. When you arrive at Harts Pass, bear right onto Slate Peak Road (FR 5400-600). At 1.5 miles, the trail takes a tight switchback to the right. This will be the exit of your hike, so if you have more than one car, it's worth dropping one of the cars off at this trailhead. Continuing onto Slate Peak, follow the road as it makes another tight turn to the left (passing Slate Pass and the trailhead for Buckskin Ridge). Follow the road to its end at the gate for Slate Peak Lookout. Look for parking spaces on the right side of the road.

GPS TRAILHEAD COORDINATES N48° 44.270' W120° 40.710'

SCENERY: ✿ ✿ ✿ ✿	TRAIL CONDITION: ✿ ✿ ✿ ✿
CHILDREN: ✿ ✿	DIFFICULTY: ✿ ✿ ✿
SOLITUDE: ✿ ✿ ✿	HIKING TIME: 2 days

DISTANCE: 19.5 miles (includes 3 miles round-trip to Windy Joe Lookout)

GREEN TRAILS MAP: *Manning Park Topo Map* (buy at Manning Park Visitor Center)

OUTSTANDING FEATURES: The northernmost point of the PCT, a great excuse to visit Canada, and a chance to stand on the highest peak in E. C. Manning Provincial Park

FOR THOSE OF YOU WHO DON'T live in Canada, this hike may seem like a haul to get to. Trust me when I tell you it's worth it. For starters, it's a loop hike, with the option to stand on top of the highest peak in E. C. Manning Provincial Park. It also starts and ends at a great swimming beach where you can also find excellent car camping to make for an extended weekend getaway. Lastly, it marks the most northern end of the Pacific Crest Trail (PCT), which is 2,659 miles from the jumping-off point in Mexico.

The sign says it all.

🚶🚶 To begin, head toward the parking lot entrance and follow the trail as it crosses an earthen dam on the east side of Spruce Bay. In a short distance, you'll come to a FROSTY MOUNTAIN sign. The main trail continues along Spruce Bay, eventually connecting up with the Lightning Lakes Trail, a mellow 12-mile (round-trip) out-and-back hike that travels along a series of four lakes. Although it's not part of the PCT, this would be a great overnight trip with kids.

Take the left branch up the Frosty Mountain Trail as it begins a steady but gentle climb through a spruce–hemlock forest. In just over a mile, the trail comes to the first of many spectacular views, with Flash and Lightning Lakes down in the valley below. Continue climbing, and at 3.2 miles, the trail gains a high point, noted as 1882 on the Manning Park map (6,000').

Around the 4-mile mark, the trail arrives at an open meadow with a sign that says CAMP with an arrow pointing down the trail. This was slightly confusing, since the actual camp was another half mile beyond the sign. Frosty Creek Camp is a large, forested site that has room for two to three tents, a fire pit with seating, a pit toilet, and a shelter. The shelter could work in a pinch; however, when I was there, it was missing a door and was unfortunately littered with trash. Frosty Creek runs along the edge of camp and is a decent water source.

To continue toward Frosty Mountain, cross Frosty Creek and begin another climb. In a half mile or so, the trail arrives at another FROSTY MOUN-TAIN sign used as a barricade to keep people off of an old trail. This also marks the entrance into what is referred to as the Larch Grove. The grade of the trail lessens as it works its way up a series of benches through gorgeous stands of alpine larches. An interpretive sign lies just off the trail around 6.5 miles and states that many of these trees are up to 3,000 years old.

Just as the trail begins to climb a narrow ridge, a spur trail breaks off to the right, heading down into a grassy meadow tucked below the north face of Frosty. This is a gorgeous spot where people obviously camp. Manning Park encourages people to camp at designated sites, but this could be an option if you wanted to camp up high. Even if you're continuing, this is a good spot to fill up water bottles, as the next main water source isn't for another 6 miles at PCT Camp.

Frosty Mountain to Windy Joe Lookout

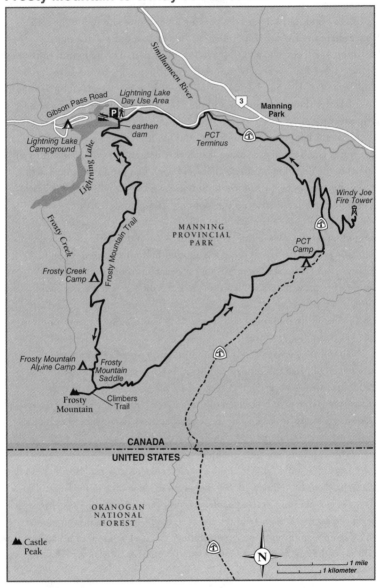

Continuing on, the trail gets steeper and more exposed as it works its way toward a large scree slope. When first arriving at the slope, the trail seems like it could be hard to follow; however, it's well traveled and fairly easy to navigate your way through. At just over 7 miles, the trail arrives at a saddle where the Windy Joe Trail drops off to the east and the summit trail climbs to the west.

If you have the energy, it's definitely worth the 30-minute side trip to the top of Frosty Mountain (7,900'). From the saddle, head west along a well-established climbers' trail to the summit, where a large, rock-walled wind shelter provides protection on blustery days. The 360-degree views are spectacular from here, with Castle Peak (8,306') to the south, Mount Spickard (8,979') to the west, Silvertip Mountain (8,517') to the north, and Mount Winthrop (7,850') to the east.

Once you have returned to the saddle, head east past a sign that warns to use extreme caution during the next section of hiking. The trail is loose and steep as it descends a series of tight switchbacks. At 1.5 miles from the saddle, the trail enters the forest, and the gradient eases off. In another 2 miles, the trail levels off at a saddle, makes a short climb, and then descends again before reaching the junction with the PCT.

You have a couple of camping options from this junction. PCT Camp is a forested camp located a half mile south on the PCT. It has a pit toilet, a fire ring, room for a couple of tents, and a small stream for water (can be dry during hot summers).

If you prefer to camp up high, you can head north on the PCT to the Windy Joe Fire Lookout. From the junction, head north on the PCT

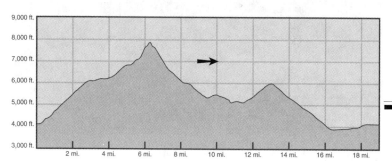

The Windy Joe Fire Lookout now serves as an interpretive site.

0.8 mile until you arrive at a signed junction for Windy Joe. The "trail" is an old service road and climbs for 1.5 miles and gains 1,000 feet of elevation. The lookout (5,988') named after Joe Hilton, one of the park's first employees and a local pioneer-trapper, was built in 1950 and was staffed until 1963. The park refurbished it and now uses it as an interpretive site. On the second level of the lookout is the original fire finder, which is mounted in the center of the room. The upper portion of the wall is covered in a panorama of the surrounding peaks, and includes names of the more prominent mountains in the area. There are no established tent sites at the lookout, but a couple of somewhat level spots are located along the ridge. There's a picnic table along with a pit toilet, but no running water, so make sure to fill up at PCT Camp before heading up.

To complete this loop, continue north from the Windy Joe junction on the PCT. The trail descends through western white pines and crosses a couple of small creeks along the way. In just over 2 miles, the trail arrives at a junction for the Windy Joe–PCT Trailhead. Stay left; the trail to the right takes you along the East Similkameen Trail.

At 3.5 miles from the Windy Joe turnoff, the trail arrives at a signed junction for the Similkameen River Trail. The trail splits to the left and right; the left branch travels along an open meadow, and the right branch parallels the south side of the road to Lightning Lake. They meet back up at the PCT–Similkameen Trailhead parking lot in less than a quarter mile. You have now arrived at the terminus of the PCT.

I'm not gonna lie—I was expecting much more. In my head, I imagined fireworks, confetti, and a cooler of cold beverages—or, at the very least, an archway or something significant to walk through. It's just a small parking lot, with room for five or so cars. I was sure the thru-hikers weren't overly concerned by the time they got to this point, so I decided I wouldn't be either. Fortunately, the rest of the hike exceeded my expectations.

From the parking lot, head west along the Little Muddy Trail. The trail name is a good indicator of what the conditions are like for the next half mile. It travels just below the road, and in a half mile arrives at a service road. Stay right here, and follow it approximately 1 mile to Twenty Minute Lake.

Continue left, and in less than half a mile, you'll arrive back at the earthen dam on the east side of Spruce Bay. Follow the trail back to the Lightning Lake Day Use Area. Hopefully, you packed your swimsuit so you can enjoy a well-deserved swim in the refreshing waters of Spruce Bay.

PERMIT No permit is required for overnight parking at the Lightning Lake Day Use Area. A backcountry permit ($5 Canadian, per person, per night) is required to camp at E. C. Manning Provincial Park. Get your permit at the visitor center 9 a.m.–6 p.m. daily, mid-June–September, or online through the BC Parks Discover Camping Reservation Service: secure.camis.com/discovercamping (choose "E. C. Manning" from pull-down menu #3 on the left). Reservations can also be made through this site for frontcountry campsites.

DIRECTIONS From downtown Seattle, take I-5 north for about 112 miles to the US–Canada border. *Note:* You must have a valid US passport, US passport card, or NEXUS card to enter Canada.

At the border, I-5 becomes British Columbia Highway 99; head north 5.8 miles on BC 99, and take Exit 10 right (north) onto King George Boulevard in Surrey. In 2.2 miles, bear right (east) onto BC 10; in another 12 miles, merge onto the Trans-Canada Highway (TCH) and drive east about 65 miles. In the town of Hope, British Columbia, the TCH heads north—continue east on BC 3 (Crowsnest Highway) and, in 3.7 miles, bear right to stay eastbound on BC 3. In about 38 miles, turn right (south) onto Gibson Pass Road in E. C. Manning Provincial Park; in another 2 miles, veer right at the fork to head toward the Lightning Lake Day Use Area. Follow the road another mile to the parking area, and park near the entrance—note that this is a popular destination, so try to get here early. Many people camp at Lightning Lake Campground the night before they head out to ensure a parking spot the next day.

GPS TRAILHEAD COORDINATES N49° 3.734' W120° 49.772'

APPENDIX A: *Park and Local Contacts*

Gifford Pinchot National Forest
www.fs.usda.gov/giffordpinchot

Forest Headquarters
10600 NE 51st Circle
Vancouver, WA 98682
360-891-5000

**Columbia River Gorge
National Scenic Area**
902 Wasco Ave., Ste. 200
Hood River, OR 97031
541-308-1700

Cowlitz Valley Ranger Station
10024 US 12/PO Box 670
Randle, WA 98377
360-497-1100

Mount Adams Ranger Station
2455 WA 141
Trout Lake, WA 98650
509-395-3400

Lake Chelan
Shuttle Service Information

Lady of the Lake (Lake Chelan Ferry)
1418 W. Woodin Ave.
Chelan, WA 98816
509-682-4584, ladyofthelake.com

Holden Shuttle
HC 0 Box 2
Chelan, WA 98816-9769
holdenvillage.org

Stehekin Shuttle
stehekin.com, info@stehekin.com

Mount Baker–Snoqualmie
National Forest
www.fs.usda.gov/mbs

Forest Headquarters
2930 Wetmore Ave., Ste. 3A
Everett, WA 98201
425-783-6000

Darrington Ranger Station
1405 Emens Ave. N.
Darrington, WA 98241
360-436-1155

Enumclaw Office
450 Roosevelt Ave. E.
Enumclaw, WA 98022
360-825-6585

North Bend Ranger Station
42404 SE North Bend Way
North Bend, WA 98045
425-888-1421

Skykomish Ranger Station
74920 NE Stevens Pass Highway/
PO Box 305
Skykomish, WA 98288
360-677-2414

Mount Rainier National Park
nps.gov/mora

Park Headquarters
55210 238th Ave. E.
Ashford, WA 98304
360-569-2211

Ohanapecosh Visitor Center
360-569-6581

Mount Rainier National Park *(continued)*

White River Wilderness Information Center
360-569-2211, ext. 6030

Okanogan-Wenatchee National Forest
www.fs.usda.gov/okawen

Forest Headquarters
215 Melody Lane
Wenatchee, WA 98801
509-664-9200

Chelan Ranger Station
428 W. Woodin Ave.
Chelan, WA 98816
509-682-2576

Cle Elum Ranger Station
803 W. Second St.
Cle Elum, WA 98922
509-852-1100

Lake Wenatchee Ranger Station
22976 WA 207
Leavenworth, WA 98826
509-763-3103

Leavenworth Ranger Station
600 Sherbourne St.
Leavenworth, WA 98826
509-548-6977

Methow Valley Ranger Station
24 W. Chewuch Road
Winthrop, WA 98862
509-996-4003

Naches Ranger Station
10237 US 12
Naches, WA 98937
509-653-1400

North Cascades National Park
nps.gov/noca

Superintendent's Office
2105 WA 20
Sedro-Woolley, WA 98284
360-856-5700

Golden West Visitor Center
PO Box 7
Stehekin, WA 98852
360-856-5700, ext. 340

Marblemount Wilderness Information Center
100 Ranger Station Road
Marblemount, WA 98267
360-854-7245

E. C. Manning Provincial Park, British Columbia, Canada
tinyurl.com/ecmanning

Visitor Center
7500 BC 3
Manning Park, BC V0X 1R0, Canada
604-668-5922

APPENDIX B: *Managing Agencies*

SOUTH: OREGON BORDER TO WHITE PASS

1 **Gillette Lake:** Columbia River Gorge National Scenic Area
2 **Bunker Hill:** Mount Adams Ranger Station, Gifford Pinchot National Forest
3 **Lemei Lake:** Mount Adams Ranger Station, Gifford Pinchot National Forest
4 **Horseshoe Meadow:** Mount Adams Ranger Station, Gifford Pinchot National Forest
5 **Nannie Ridge:** Cowlitz Valley Ranger Station, Gifford Pinchot National Forest
6 **Old Snowy Mountain:** Naches Ranger Station, Okanogan-Wenatchee National Forest
7 **Round Mountain:** Cowlitz Valley Ranger Station, Gifford Pinchot National Forest

CENTRAL: WHITE PASS TO STEVENS PASS

8 **Buesch and Dumbbell Lakes:** Cowlitz Valley and Naches Ranger Stations, Gifford Pinchot National Forest
9 **Laughingwater Creek:** White River Wilderness Information Center, Mount Rainier National Park
10 **Dewey Lake:** White River Wilderness Information Center, Mount Rainier National Park; Naches Ranger District, Okanogan-Wenatchee National Forest
11 **Sheep Lake and Sourdough Gap:** Naches Ranger District, Okanogan-Wenatchee National Forest
12 **Bullion Basin to Silver Creek:** Enumclaw Office, Mount Baker–Snoqualmie National Forest
13 **Big Crow Basin:** Enumclaw Office, Mount Baker–Snoqualmie National Forest
14 **Mirror Lake:** Cle Elum Ranger Station, Okanogan-Wenatchee National Forest
15 **Commonwealth Basin to Red Pass:** North Bend Ranger Station, Mount Baker–Snoqualmie National Forest
16 **Kendall Katwalk:** North Bend Ranger Station, Mount Baker–Snoqualmie National Forest
17 **Spectacle Lake:** Cle Elum Ranger Station, Okanogan-Wenatchee National Forest
18 **Cathedral and Deception Passes:** Cle Elum Ranger Station, Okanogan-Wenatchee National Forest
19 **Surprise and Glacier Lakes:** Skykomish Ranger Station, Mount Baker–Snoqualmie National Forest
20 **Hope and Mig Lakes:** Skykomish Ranger Station, Mount Baker–Snoqualmie National Forest
21 **Chain and Doelle Lakes:** Leavenworth Ranger Station, Okanogan-Wenatchee National Forest

NORTH: STEVENS PASS TO CANADIAN BORDER

22 **Lake Valhalla:** Skykomish Ranger Station, Mount Baker–Snoqualmie National Forest
23 **Cady Ridge to Kodak Peak:** Lake Wenatchee Ranger Station, Okanogan-Wenatchee National Forest
24 **Little Giant Pass:** Lake Wenatchee Ranger Station, Okanogan-Wenatchee National Forest

(Continued on next page)

25 Suiattle River to Miners Ridge, Including Image Lake: Darrington Ranger Station, Mount Baker–Snoqualmie National Forest

26 Lyman Lakes and Suiattle Pass: Chelan Ranger Station, Okanogan-Wenatchee National Forest

27 Agnes Creek: Golden West Visitor Center, Chelan Ranger Station, North Cascades National Park

28 Rainbow Lake and McAlester Creek: Marblemount Wilderness Information Center, North Cascades National Park; Methow Valley Ranger Station, Okanogan-Wenatchee National Forest

29 Cutthroat Pass: Methow Valley Ranger Station, Okanogan-Wenatchee National Forest

30 Grasshopper Pass: Methow Valley Ranger Station, Okanogan-Wenatchee National Forest

31 Tamarack Peak: Methow Valley Ranger Station, Okanogan-Wenatchee National Forest

32 West Fork Pasayten to PCT: Methow Valley Ranger Station, North Cascades National Park

33 Frosty Mountain to Windy Joe Lookout: Manning Park Visitor Center, E. C. Manning Provincial Park

INDEX

Page references followed by *m* indicate a map.

ABOUT THE AUTHOR

ADRIENNE SCHAEFER began loving nature and outdoor pursuits at a young age, when she built forts and camped out with her family in the foothills of Washington's North Cascades. As she got older, her love turned into a lifestyle, and she decided to pursue a career in the outdoor industry.

PHOTO: DONNI VOGNILD

A bachelor's degree in outdoor recreation led Adrienne to a variety of outdoor-based jobs, including working for the National Park Service and the U.S. Forest Service as a trail crew member, a wildland firefighter, and a climbing ranger on Mount Rainier. She spent her winters chasing powder and working odd jobs until she eventually landed a job as a professional ski patroller for Stevens Pass Ski Area. She has since settled in the Methow Valley, where she now works as a backcountry ski guide for North Cascades Mountain Guides.

When Adrienne isn't working, she roams the high country of the North Cascades or spends time at home, where she enjoys trail running, gardening, and hanging out with her husband, John; their two boys, Tye and Reid; and their dog, Lemah.